Collins

Cascade 2

A SKILL-BASED COURSE IN ENVIRONMENTAL STUDIES

Series Editor
Padmini Sriraman

Components of DigiSuite

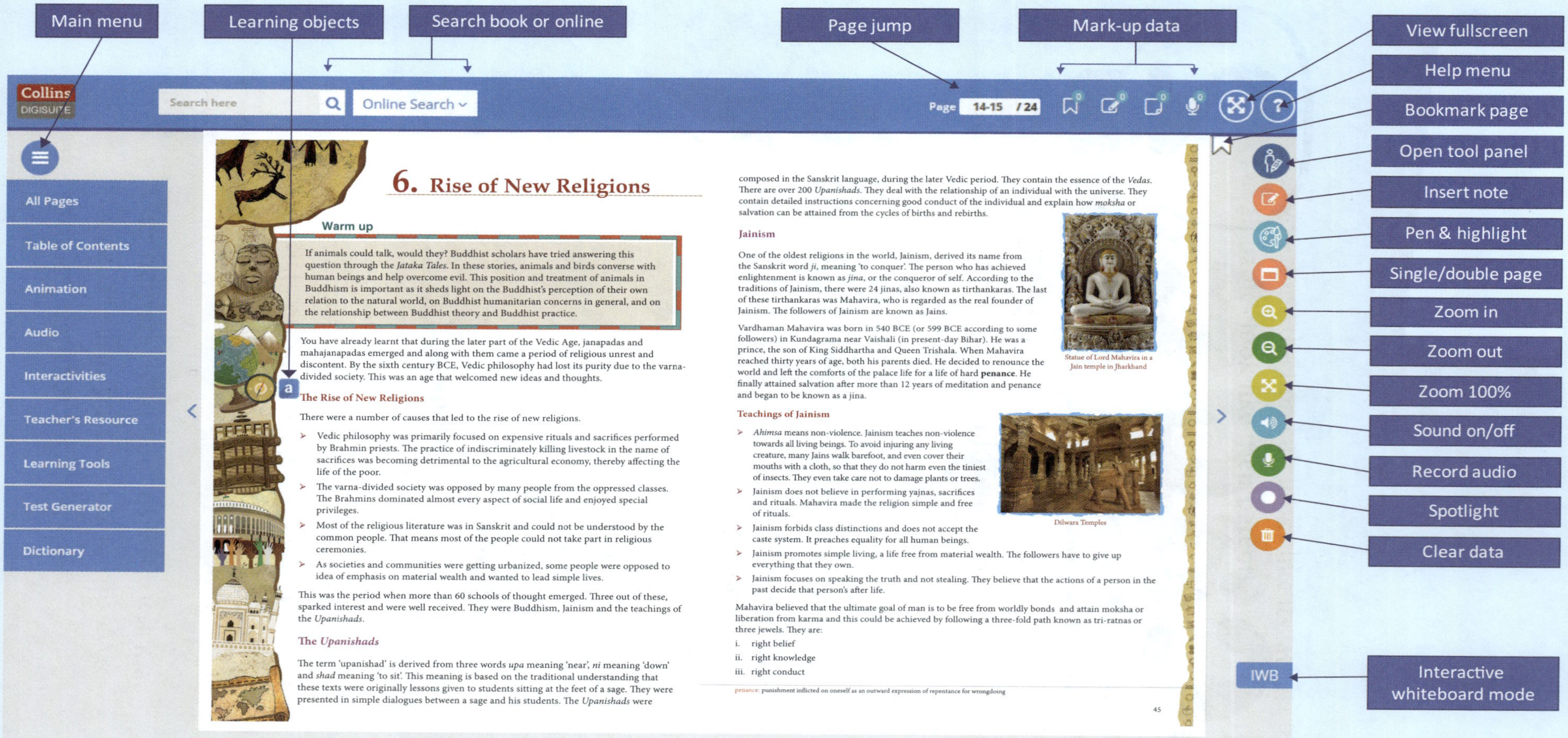

Student + Teacher			Teacher-only	
a animations	ia activities	g games	lp lesson plans	tn teacher's notes
ilt instructor-led tutorials	w worksheets	v videos	w worksheets	ak answer keys
	audio			

Preface

Cascade is a skill-based course on Environmental Studies and Social Studies for the foundational, preparatory and middle stages. This series for classes 1 to 8 is aligned to the National Education Policy, 2020. Taking into account the multidisciplinary nature of Environmental Studies and Social Studies, the series follows an interactive approach through a variety of tasks and stimulating content. This series deals with the study of human behaviour, relationships, resources and institutions in local as well as global contexts, all of which are fundamental to our conception of society.

Cascade and the NEP

Based on an interactive pedagogy, the books focus on:

- Conceptual development encouraging students to learn how to learn through Constructivist learning tasks
- Thinking critically, solving problems and learning essential life skills to imbibe 21st century learning
- Creative skills aimed at developing all capabilities of learners and to increase individual happiness from childhood
- Multidisciplinary teaching which aligns to the NIPUN initiative for young learners
- Inquiring, analyzing and absorbing new information in a world of increasing interconnections through inferential and experiential tasks
- Sustainable Development Goals that hold the key to the future of mankind sensitizing young learners through a gradual study that builds environmental and social awareness
- The promotion of Indian arts and culture to inculcate a sense of identity as well as an appreciation of other cultures and identities
- Competency-based Structured Assessments For Analyzing Learning (SAFAL)

About the series editor

Padmini Sriraman, has worked in the field of education for more than four decades. She was the former Principal of The Hindu Senior Secondary School in Chennai. A recipient of the CBSE National Award, Padmini is an author, consultant, mentor, master trainer CBSE and resource person of COE CBSE Chennai. She has conducted many workshops and seminars for teachers and principals across India and abroad.

KEY FEATURES

Cascade offers features that focus on essential skills to assist learners achieve holistic learning through a multidisciplinary approach. In so doing, the series is aligned with the guidelines given in the National Education Policy, 2020.

Learning

Warm up

Why do some places on our planet have summer season while others have winter season?
The Earth, like all the planets of our solar system, revolves around the Sun, and hence is not stationary. Though we may not be able to feel its movement, these movements causes day and night or summer and winter.

Warm up has pre-reading tasks for discovery-based learning

Conceptual Development

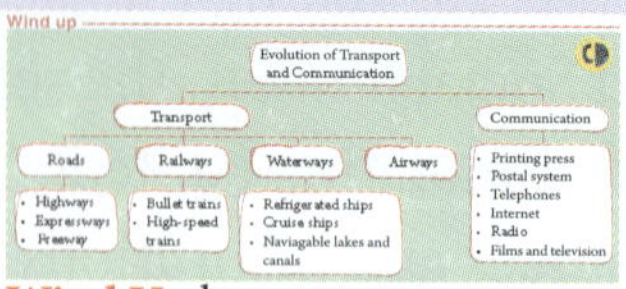

Wind Up has concept maps to assist in learning

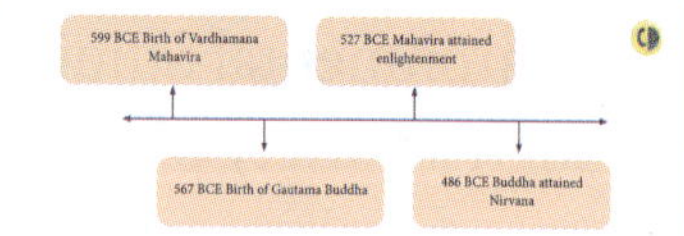

Timeline helps learners understand the chronology of events

Extended learning

Skill Builder

Critical thinking skills: What happens if we burn leaves and twigs? What should we do instead of this?
Communication skills: Discuss in class why the action shown in the picture is incorrect.
Life skills: Talk to the gardener of your neighbourhood park. Find out how he takes care of the plants.
Creativity and innovation skills:
Look at the picture. How can you help the bird which has lost its home?

Skill builder has 21st century skills necessary in the age of information

Connect

Growing children must follow a daily routine. They should eat well and sleep on time to let their body grow.

Connect highlights stories and events from around the world related to the chapter.

FACT CHECK

Plants need air, water, sunlight and soil. They can make their own food.

Fact check provides interesting titbits of information

Green Earth

Trees are cut down to make paper. Therefore, we should not waste paper.

Green Earth sensitizes learners towards conservation of the environment.

Constructivist learning

Learning Tools

Complete the following chart to make your own study material:

Globes	Maps	Types of maps

Components of a map	New terms
Scale Directions Symbols Colours	

Learning Tools are student-made study guides to organize and arrange data encouraging self learning

Creativity and happiness

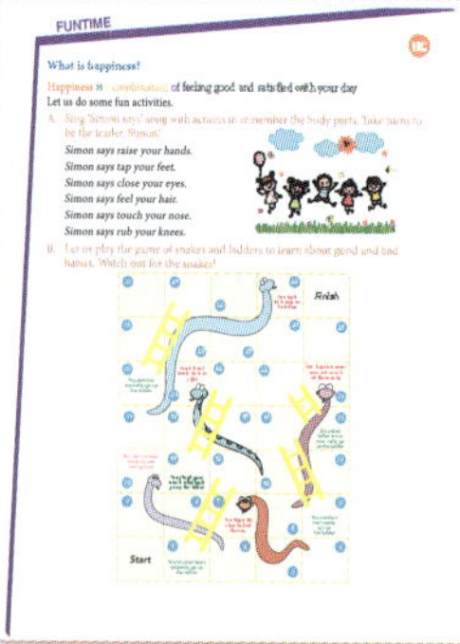

Fun Time addresses wellbeing and happiness of the students through creative and fun tasks

SDG Posters encourage sustainable living

Cross-curricular learning

What's in the picture?

Look at the family picnic picture. Name the sense organ that is being used by each person.

Mother:......................

Girl with dog:..........................

Father:..........................

Boy:.........................

Girl:..........................

What's in the picture? provides exercises for inferential learning

SAFAL

Geography skills

Use an atlas to find out the climatic zones in which the following countries are located:

1. India 2. United Kingdom
3. Finland 4. Kenya
5. South Africa 6. New Zealand

SAFAL

Geography skills build map skills and improve world overview of learners

Think Big — Data Fun

Hailey asked her friends about their favourite colour. She showed their answers by drawing circles in a table.

FAVORITE COLORS	
Colour	Number of likes
Red	●●●
Blue	●●●●●
Yellow	●
Green	●●●
Purple	●●●●

How many of Hailey's friends chose blue as their favorite color?

Find out the favourite colour of 10-15 students in your class from the given choices. Draw coloured stars to show their answers in the table.

Colour	Number of students
Pink	★
Orange	
Brown	
Yellow	
Green	

Say, how many of your friends chose green as their favourite colour.

Think Big provides varied activities for multidisciplinary learning

Observation and application

Apply it!

Look at the pictures. Write how the child is feeling.

....

Apply it! provides application-based activities for experiential learning

The Sahus

The Sahus have three children, Ajay, Sara and baby Raju. Mr. Sahu is a mason. He works hard to earn money and take care of his family. Ajay goes to school. But Sara needs to be at home to help her mother and to look after baby Raju. In the evening Ajay goes out to play with his friends but Sara does not as her mother asks her to look after her younger baby brother while she cooks for the family.

- Who all are there in the Sahu family?
- Do you think the children are treated equally? Discuss.
- Should Sara go to school?

Case Study re-counts in-depth investigations of a single person, group, event or community.

SAFAL

Assessment and practice

Exercises

A. Choose the correct answer to fill in the blanks.

1. .... is at the centre of the solar system.
   a. Mars b. Sun c. Earth
2. .... is the fifth planet from Earth.
   a. Mercury b. Jupiter c. Neptune

ASSESSMENT 1

A. Choose the correct option to fill in the blanks.

1. We live with our ______________
   a. friends b. family c. neighbours
2. We use our hands to ______________
   a. write b. kick c. run
3. We must wear a mask while going out as it ______________
   a. protects from pollution b. is fashion c. protects from illness
4. Our classrooms should be ______________
   a. dusty b. clean c. dark
5. A ______________ looks after us when we are sick.
   a. cleaner b. maid c. nurse

B. Write T for true and F for false sentences.

1. An identity card tells us nothing about the person wearing it.
2. Exercise keeps us fit for the whole day.
3. We must share work with our family members.
4. We can throw papers in the classroom.
5. Houses can be kutcha or pucca.

SAFAL

Exercises, **Assessments** and **Outline Maps** for assessment

Contents

1. I Am Me!

Warm up

Fill in the blanks with information about yourself.
Draw and colour your face in the box.

- My name is ....
- My hair is .... (long/short).
- I write with my .... (left/right) hand.
- I .... (wear/do not wear) spectacles.
- I like to .... and ....

Have you seen photos of yourself as a baby? Are you different now? With age, we become bigger and grow older. This is called growing up. All babies grow up into a toddler, teenager, adult and old person.

Growing up

I Can Do

As we grow older, we learn new things. There are some things that we can start doing by ourselves.

What's in the picture?

Tick (✓) the things that you can do on your own.

☐ ☐ ☐ ☐

I Am Special

We may be the same as our friends in some ways. We study in the same class. We are of the same age. But we like different things. We all look different from one another. Each one of us is **special**.

Do you have any **similarities** with any of your family members?

> **FACT CHECK**
> Some twins look alike. But even twins have different likes and dislikes.

Hobbies

We all like to do some activities for pleasure when we are not working. Such an activity is called a hobby. Different people have different hobbies.

Singing

Dancing

Solving puzzles

Reading

Swimming

Cycling

Sometimes, we feel **differently** too. There are things that make us happy and things that make us sad. We should take care of ourselves to remain healthy.

> **Green Earth**
> Grow a plant in your house and give it a pet name.

special: different from others; similarities: things that make us the same as other people; differently: to not be the same as others

Apply it!

Look at the pictures. Write how the child is feeling.

....

Skill Builder

Critical thinking skills: You know that each person is special. Find out how your friends differ from one another and fill in the table.

Special Things	Friend's Name
Tallest	
Thinnest	
Quietest	
Always smiling	

Life skills and values: Posture is the way we stand or sit. A good posture makes us look smart. Tick (✓) the things you follow for a good posture:

1. Hold your head up while standing. ☐
2. Keep your feet on the table while sitting. ☐
3. Pull your shoulders back while standing. ☐
4. Keep your back straight against the backrest while sitting. ☐

Information literacy: Everyone has unique fingerprints. Find out what fingerprints are.

Connect

Growing children must follow a daily routine. They should eat well and sleep on time to let their body grow.

Wind up

- As we grow older, we learn new things.
- Each one of us is special.
- Different people have different hobbies.

Exercises

A. Choose the correct word from the box to fill in the blanks.

different	ourselves	special	learn	taller

1. We .... new things every day.
2. We look .... from our friends.
3. We are all ....
4. We can do some things by ....
5. We grow .... as we grow up.

B. Write how you feel, whether happy or sad, in these instances.

1. Eating an ice cream ....
2. Getting hurt while playing ....
3. Singing on stage ....
4. Painting and drawing ....

C. Answer in one word.

1. What is becoming older and bigger called? ....
2. Name any one similarity you have with your parents. ....
3. When is your birthday? ....
4. Name one of your hobbies. ....

Think Big

Art integration

Make a photo frame.

Material required: lolly sticks , ribbon, glue and glitter or stars

Method:

1. Take four lolly sticks and paint them. Paste them together as shown.
2. Stick a ribbon on the backside of the frame and decorate it with glitter, stars or bindi.
3. Then, paste your photo on it and hang it in your room.

Learning Tools

Look at the pictures given in each row and circle the odd one out!

1. 

2. 

3. 

4. 

5. 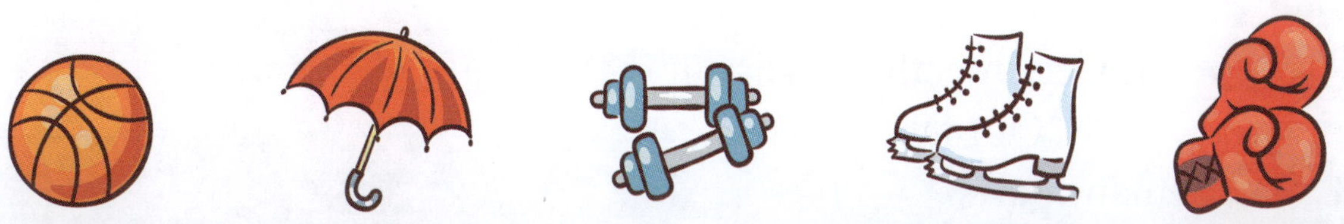

Web links:

https://www.bbc.co.uk/learningenglish/english/features/childrens-stories
https://www.dkfindout.com/uk/human-body/life-cycle/childhood/

Last accessed on 30 August 2021

2. Our Body

Warm up

Have you ever played the game - Blind man's buff? How are you able to catch the other players if your eyes are closed?

Parts of Our Body

Our body helps us to do many activities. It has different parts. The parts of the body that have particular functions are known as organs. Our body has three types of organs—external organs, sense organs and internal organs.

External Organs

The parts of the body that are outside and can be seen by us are called external organs. Our head, neck, hands, chest, legs and feet are external organs. Our arms and legs together form our limbs. Our face also has many parts.

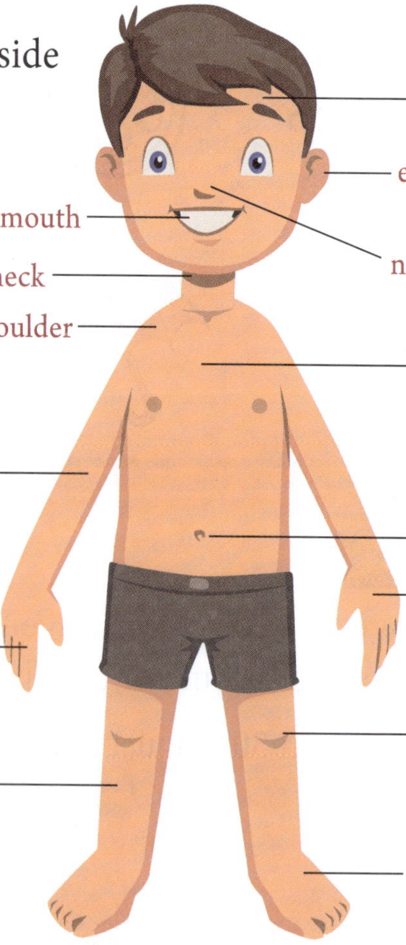

External organs

FACT CHECK

Fins help fish to swim. Their tail helps them to change direction.

Sense Organs

We have five **senses**. These are sense of taste, **sight**, hearing, smell and touch. We use our sense organs to sense them.

- Our eyes help us to see things around us.
- Our ears help us to hear sounds.
- Our nose helps us to smell things. It also helps us to breathe.
- Our tongue is in our mouth. It helps us to taste things and speak.
- Our skin helps us to touch and feel things.

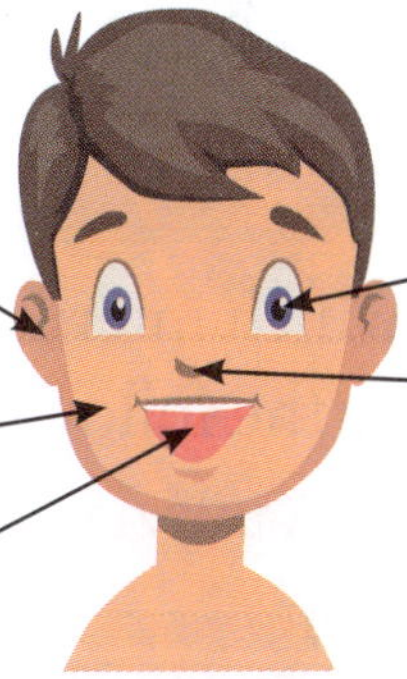

Sense organs

What's in the picture?

Look at the family picnic picture. Name the sense organ that is being used by each person.

1. Mother: ....
2. Girl with dog: ....
3. Father: ....
4. Boy: ....
5. Toddler: ....

Internal Organs

We have some parts of the body that we cannot see. These are inside our body and are called internal organs. The heart, brain, lungs and stomach are some of the internal organs. Each part plays a special role.

Our brain is inside our head. It helps us to think. It also controls all the other organs of the body.

Touch the left side of your chest. Do you feel something **beating**? This is the heart. The heart pumps blood to all parts of our body.

Green Earth

Some plants respond to touch. The leaves of the Mimosa plant, also called 'touch me not plant', droop if one touches them.

sense: the ability to taste, touch, see, smell and hear; sight: the ability to see things with our eyes
beating: the sound that our heart makes

Inside our chest, we have lungs. Lungs help us to breathe. Lungs come in a pair, like our hands and legs.

All the food that we eat goes to our stomach. The stomach helps us to **digest** food.

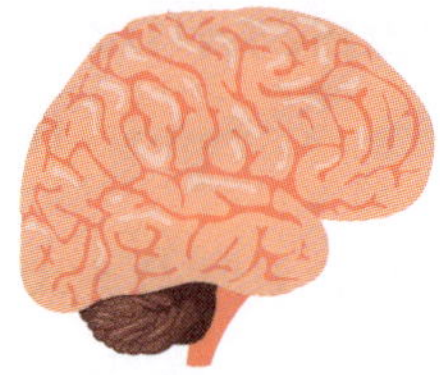

Brain

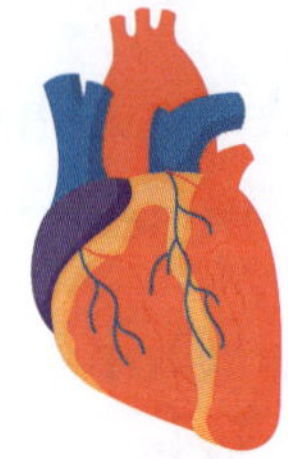

Heart

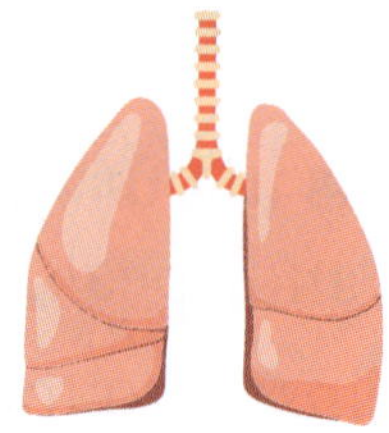

Lungs

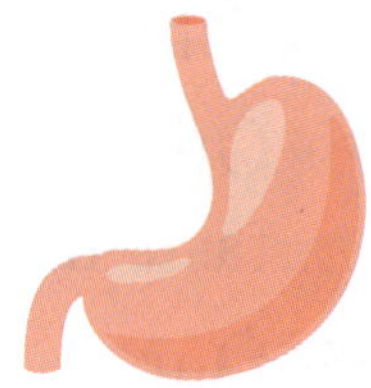

Stomach

Apply it! E

Write which internal organ will help in doing the following activities.

1. Solve a puzzle ....
2. Breathe ....
3. Digest food ....
4. Pump blood ....

Bones and Muscles

Touch and press your knees, fingers and elbows. Do you feel something hard? These hard parts are our bones. Now, touch and press your arms and belly. Do you feel something soft? The soft parts are muscles.

Bones give support to our body and make us strong. Muscles help us move. They both give a shape to our body and help it to function. They protect the internal organs. Bones and muscles are covered by our skin.

Healthy Body

As we grow older, our body changes. We become bigger, taller and we start doing many things that we could not do when we were younger.

We should take good care of our body. For good health and well-being, we must eat healthy food, drink lots of water, exercise regularly and take rest. We must stand and sit straight to have a good posture. Let us look at some good habits we should follow to stay healthy.

Green Earth

Walking to school not only keeps the body fit and healthy but also helps in keeping the air clean.

digest: breaking down of food in the stomach

Wake up early in the morning and go to sleep early.

Brush our teeth every morning and at night before going to bed.

Eat healthy food.[*]

Bathe every day and wear neat and clean clothes.

Exercise and play in a park every day.

Wash our hands before and after eating our meals.

Sit straight to have a good posture.

Follow the new normal rules in school and at play to remain safe during the **pandemic**.

Wear face mask and maintain distance

* The Sustainable Development Goals (SDGs) are 17 global goals adopted by the United Nations in 2015. This is a universal call to all nations for action to end inequality, poverty, protect the planet and ensure that by 2030 all people enjoy peace and prosperity.

pandemic: an occurrence of a disease that affects many people over a very wide area

Skill Builder

21ST CENTURY SKILLS

Critical thinking skills: Take this sense organ quiz.

1. Which animal uses the sense of smell to hunt things?
2. Which bird can see clearly at night?
3. Which animal has a strong sense of hearing?

Life skills:

1. Tick (✓) the actions that you should do to take care of your body:
   a. Exercise daily ☐
   b. Insert pencil in the ear ☐
   c. Clean the tongue ☐
   d. Eat unhealthy food often ☐
2. Sara fell down the stairs while running and fractured her leg.
   a. Will you be friendly to her?
   b. Is it right to run down the stairs?
   c. Which games will you play with her now?

10 REDUCED INEQUALITIES

Connect

We must take care of our skin as it is our body's largest organ.

Wind up

- Our body helps us to do many activities.
- We have five sense organs.
- Our body has external organs and internal organs.
- Bones and muscles together give shape to our body.
- We must take good care of our body.

Exercises

A. Choose the correct option to fill in the blanks.

1. Our .... is found inside the body.
   a. hand b. heart c. hair

2. Our .... helps us to taste food.

a. tongue b. ear c. eye

3. Our .... helps us to digest the food we eat.

a. lungs b. stomach c. legs

4. Our .... helps us to think.

a. eye b. brain c. legs

5. Our .... give support to our body.

a. bones b. stomach c. muscles

B. Write T for True and F for False.

1. Our stomach helps us to breathe. ☐
2. We should always sit straight. ☐
3. We smell with our tongue. ☐
4. We must wash our hands before and after eating our meals. ☐
5. We must not chew food and eat. ☐

C. Answer in one word.

1. What are arms and legs called together? ....
2. What helps the body to move? ....
3. Which organ in our body helps us to breathe? ....

Think Big

Science Fun

Let us do an activity. Take a glass. Pour a little squash in it. Then, pour cold water and stir with a spoon. Listen to the sound of the spoon touching the glass while stirring. Smell the squash and taste the drink.

Name the organs that helped you to:

1. see the things needed to make the drink ....
2. feel whether the water is cold or not ....
3. listen to the clinking sound of the spoon moving in the glass ....
4. smell the squash ....
5. taste the drink ....

Learning Tools

Look at the picture and the numbers of the body parts. Now complete the crossword.

Across: 2, 3, 4, 5, 10, 11, 12 Down: 1, 6, 7, 8, 9

Web links:

https://kids.nationalgeographic.com/weird-but-true/article/humanbody2
https://www.dkfindout.com/uk/
Last accessed on 30 August 2021

Stay safe

Follow these safety rules to stay safe during a pandemic:

- Cover your cough or sneeze with your sleeve or disposable tissue.
- Don't touch eyes, nose or mouth without washing your hands.
- Wear a mask when you go out and use a sanitizer.
- Do not shake hands with others.
- Maintain social distance from others.
- If you feel sick or have fever, stay home.
- Stay at home and go out only if necessary.

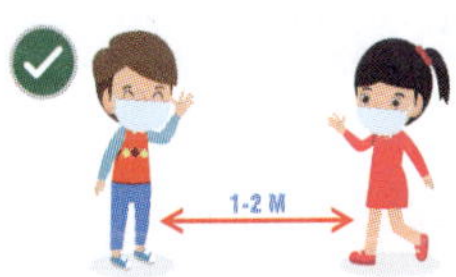

Steps to wash hands properly:

1. 
Use soap

2. 
Palm to palm

3. 
Back of hands

4. 
Fingers interlaced

5. 
Rinse hands

6. 
Dry hands

3. Family Time

Warm up

Do you think the lion cub looks like its father?
Do all babies look like their parents?

Types of Families

Families are of different kinds. Some are small and some are large. A small family has parents and children living together. It is known as a nuclear family.

A nuclear family

A joint family

A large family has parents, children and grandparents living together. In some large families, even uncles, aunts and cousins live with the family. Such a large family is known as a joint family.

A one-parent family

Some children live with one parent, either mother or father. A family that consists of one parent and his or her children living together, is called a one-parent family.

Our helpers, who help us with work at home, are also part of our family. We should treat them with respect.

Our helpers

Relations

Our family members are our relatives. Our sisters and brothers are our siblings. Our mother's parents are our **maternal** grandparents. Our father's parents are our **paternal** grandparents.

> ✓ FACT CHECK
>
> Elephants live with their babies in family groups called herds.

The brothers and sisters of our parents are our uncles and aunts. Their children are our cousins. We keep in touch with our relatives and meet them during festivals, vacations, weddings and other **occasions**. Family members help one another.

Apply it!

Hi, I am Benu. Look at the members of my family in this family tree.

Circle the relatives from my mother's side and tick (✓) the relatives from my father's side.

Fun with Family

All the members of a family have fun together. They enjoy at home by playing games and watching TV together. They celebrate festivals, go out for picnics and visit people and other places together. Family members love and care for one another.

> **Green Earth**
>
> Use paper bags and cloth bags when you go shopping.

maternal: related through the mother's side of the family; paternal: related through the father's side of the family; occasion: an important event, ceremony or celebration

Look at some ways in which families have fun together.

Having meals together

Going on a road trip

Going on family picnics

Going to shopping mall

Visiting relatives

Going to amusement parks

What's in the picture?

Tick (✓) the things that you can do to help your family members.

1. 

Leave your toys and clothes lying all over the room

2. 

Put your dirty clothes in the laundry basket

3. 

Sit and play games all day

4. 

Carry your own plate for washing after every meal

Skill Builder

21ST CENTURY SKILLS

Critical thinking skills: How do you feel when your family members thank you for helping them?

Life skills: Fill in the blanks with the correct answers:

1. Misha's mother has a sister whose name is Avni. Avni is Misha's ....
   a. brother b. aunt c. cousin d. grandmother
2. Aman and Sana have a daughter named Sara. Sara has a sister named Sania. Sania is Sara's ....
   a. cousin b. grandfather c. sibling d. brother

Collaboration skills: What types of families do two of your friends have?
Communication skills: In what ways do you help your family with the household work? Discuss in class.
Creativity: Make a scrapbook with your pictures while having fun with your family members.

Connect

15 May is celebrated as the International Day of Families.

Wind up

- There are different types of families—nuclear families, joint families and one-parent families.
- The members of a family help one another.
- Our family members are our relatives.
- We have fun with our family. Family members love and care for one another.

Exercises

A. Choose the correct option to fill in the blanks.

1. Our sisters and brothers are our ....
   a. siblings b. friends c. aunts
2. A large family with uncles, aunts and cousins is called a .... family.
   a. nuclear b. joint c. one-parent
3. My maternal grandmother is my .... mother.
   a. mother's b. father's c. sister's
4. The members of a family..................... one another.
   a. ignore b. help c. trouble

B. Write which family member helps you do the following things.

1. Takes you out for fun activities ....
2. Teaches you things ....
3. Makes you laugh ....

C. Answer in one word.

1. What is a family with just parents and children known as? ....
2. Which word includes all family members? ....
3. Name your favourite way of having fun with your family. ....

Think Big

Crafts Fun

Let's make a duck family.

Material required: yellow and orange coloured paper, a black marker, a pencil, colours, scissors and glue

Method:

1. Trace your hand and your mother and father's hand onto a yellow sheet of paper. Ask them to help you cut out the hand prints. Cut out circles to make head of the ducks.
2. Glue the duck's heads to the thumb of the hand prints.
3. Cut out small triangles from an orange sheet of paper, to make the beaks. Paste the beaks halfway on the edge of the heads.
4. Draw the eyes above the beak using a black marker.
5. Cut out the legs separately and paste them at the bottom of the hand print ducks. Your duck family is ready!

Learning Tools

Tick (✓) the activities you do with your grandparents. Talk to your grandparents and find out more about their childhood.

1.

2.

3.

4.

Web links:

https://kids.nationalgeographic.com/weird-but-true/article/family-facts

Last accessed on 30 August 2021

4. Houses People Live In

Warm up

Which room is this in a house? What can you do here?

We need a house for **shelter** and safety. A house protects us from heat, wind, cold, rain and animals. The house we live in with our family is our home.

Types of Houses

Multi-storied apartments

Houses can be **temporary** or **permanent**. Kutcha houses are temporary houses while pucca houses are permanent ones. Most cities have pucca houses like bungalows and multi-storied apartments. Kutcha houses are mostly found in the villages. These are built with mud, straw and bamboo. The pucca houses are made with cement, bricks and stones.

Temporary Houses

A tent

People who move from one place to another live in temporary houses. Tents, caravans and houseboats are temporary houses. Tents are made from a thick cloth, called canvas, or from plastic sheets. They can be folded and carried along from one place to another.

shelter: a place that covers or gives protection; temporary: lasting for a very short time; permanent: lasting for a long time or for all the time

FACT CHECK

A tepee is a tall tent, shaped like a cone.

Caravans are houses built on wheels. There is a place to sleep, a washroom and a small kitchen.

A caravan

Houseboats are floating houses built with wood.

A houseboat

Houses in Different Places

People living in different places build different types of houses according to the climate of the place.

A stilt house

Igloos are snow houses built in extremely cold places. They have a round roof and a very small entrance.

An igloo

People in the areas that receive heavy rains build houses raised on wooden pillars or **stilts**. These are called stilt houses.

Houses in the hilly areas are built with wood and stones. Such houses keep people warm.

What's in the picture?

Look at the pictures of different houses. Match them with their names.

1. 
2. 
3. 
4. 

a. Cottage b. Castle c. Farmhouse d. Treehouse

Types of Roofs

Sloping roof

Flat roof

The top of a house is known as a roof. Roofs can be flat or **sloping**. In places with heavy rains and snow, houses have sloping roofs so that rainwater or snow can easily slide down and not collect on the roof. In warm areas that do not have much rainfall, houses have flat roofs.

stilts: a set of posts supporting a building; sloping: being higher at one end than the other

People Who Build Houses

Many people work together to build a house. These include plumber, carpenter, mason, **architect** and electrician.

Apply it!

Fill in the letters to name the people who work at a construction site.

- An A R .... I .... C ...... plans a house.
- A P .... N .... R paints the house.
- A P L ...... M .... lays down pipes and fittings in bathrooms.
- A M ...... S ...... N lays bricks and builds the foundation and walls.
- An E L .... T .... C .... N lays wires and fits fans and lights.
- A .... R P ...... N .... makes the windows and doors of the house.

A Clean House

It is important to keep our house neat and clean to stay healthy. We should:

- dust our home regularly
- use a covered bin for garbage
- keep windows open for fresh air and sunlight

A clean house

Green Earth

A good house has windows to let fresh air in. This keeps the house cool and fresh.

architect: a person who makes the plan for a building

Skill Builder

21st CENTURY SKILLS

Critical thinking skills: Why do we find multi-storied apartments in most cities?

Communication skills: What do you feel about animal shelters that keep animals locked up? Do you think it is good for the animals?

Life skills: Where should I live? Name the type of houses for each.

1. I have to live at a place where it rains a lot. ....
2. I have to stay in a snow-bound area. ....
3. I have to stay in a village near the fields. ....
4. I have to be on the road so I need a house with wheels. ....

Information literacy: Tick (✓) the materials required to make a pucca house.

sand	☐	grass	☐	brick	☐
cement	☐	steel	☐	canvas	☐

Connect

We must grow more plants and trees around our home, as they give out fresh air.

Wind up

- Houses provide us with shelter and safety.
- Houses can be temporary or permanent.
- People living in different places build different types of houses.
- There are different people who help in building houses.
- We should keep our house clean.

Exercises

A. Choose the correct option to fill in the blanks.

1. A house keeps us safe from ....
   a. rain b. animals c. both of these
2. A tent is made of ....
   a. cement b. bamboo c. canvas

3. The houses found in very cold places are called ....

a. stilt houses   b. huts   c. igloos

4. Places where it is hot and rains less have .... type of roof.

a. sloping   b. flat   c. glass

5. Adequate .... in a house help the people to stay healthy.

a. sunlight   b. clothes   c. rains

B. Write Yes or No.

1. A clean house keeps us healthy. ....
2. A temporary house is built with bricks. ....
3. A houseboat is made using mud. ....
4. Some houses have sloping roofs so that rainwater or snow easily slides down. ....
5. An architect builds a house. ....

C. Answer in one word.

1. What does a home provide us? ....
2. What are permanent houses made of? ....
3. Name a floating house built with wood. ....

Think Big — Craft Fun

Make a paper house.

Material required: paper, a pair of scissors, sketch pens and glue

Method:

1. Fold a sheet of paper in half to make a crease.
2. Fold from both sides to meet the crease line.

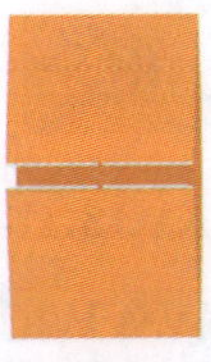

3. Fold along the dotted lines shown here.

4. Fold back, open and flatten it.

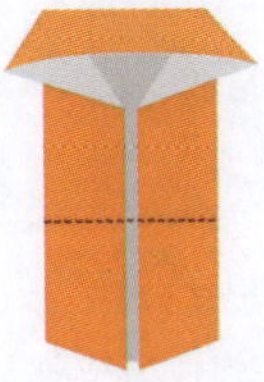

5. You can draw doors and windows to complete the house.

Learning Tools

Create your own notes for the chapter in the format given below.

TYPES OF ROOFS

PEOPLE WHO BUILD HOUSE

TEMPORARY HOUSES

HOUSES IN DIFFERENT PLACES

CLEAN HOUSE

Web links:

https://kids.nationalgeographic.com/awesome-8/article/wacky-houses
https://www.dkfindout.com/uk/history/native-americans/inuit/

Last accessed on 30 August 2021

WORKSHEET

Worksheet (Chapters 1-4)

A. Choose the correct option to fill in the blanks.

1. As we grow older we become ....
   a. younger　b. taller　c. shorter
2. Parts of the body that perform a specific function are called ....
   a. organs　b. muscles　c. bones
3. .... are houses built in extremely cold places.
   a. Caravan　b. Tent　c. Igloo
4. Our family members are our ....
   a. friends　b. teachers　c. relatives
5. Pucca houses are made up of ....
   a. bricks　b. mud　c. straw
6. Places where it rains a lot have houses with .... roofs.
   a. steel　b. sloping　c. flat
7. .... is an internal body organ.
   a. Brain　b. Neck　c. Feet
8. My mother's father is my ....
   a. uncle　b. paternal grandfather　c. maternal grandfather

B. Match the body parts to the actions.

1. 
2. 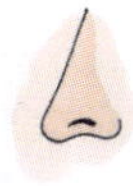
3. 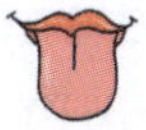
4. 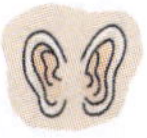
5. 

a. 
b. 
c. 
d. 
e. 

C. Fill in the blanks.

1. Huts are also known as ....
2. We call our brother and sister our ....
3. Floating houses are called ....
4. Different people have .... hobbies.
5. Skin helps us to .... and ....
6. A family consisting of parents and children only is called a .... family.

5. Our Neighbourhood

Warm up

Look at the picture and talk about it.

- Identify this place and name it.
- Do you have it in your neighbourhood?
- Why do people go here?

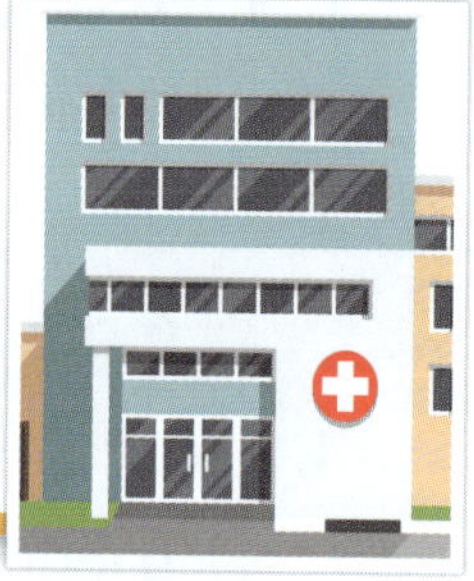

There are many places in our neighbourhood. These places help make our lives comfortable.

Many neighbourhoods have a bank. We keep our money and **costly** things in a bank. Banks keep them safe for us. There are also a few ATMs located in and around a neighbourhood.

Bank

When people need to board a bus to go somewhere, they stand and wait at the bus stop. Big cities like Delhi are connected by a metro. People go to the petrol pump to get fuel for their vehicles. Some neighbourhoods have a pharmacy, which is a store that sells medicines.

Pharmacy

Petrol pump

Metro station

Bus stop

costly: of great price

Big neighbourhoods have hospitals and fire stations. Fire stations have firefighters, fire brigades and things that are needed to put out fires.

Some neighbourhoods also have places like a greengrocer, shopping mall and a school or a hotel.

One can find a temple, gurdwara, mosque or a church in a neighbourhood too. Many of these places become **landmarks**, which help us to locate a place easily.

What's in the picture?

- Identify this place.
- Why do we go here?
- Name two things that we would find here.

Fire station

Greengrocer

FACT CHECK

A fire engine carries firefighters, hoses, water tanks, masks, first aid kit and high ladders to put out fire.

Taking Care of the Neighbourhood

We should always keep our neighbourhood clean. We should be friendly with our neighbours. We must help our neighbours, especially the elderly, in times of need.

Green Earth

Always throw waste inside the dustbin to keep your neighbourhood clean.

During a pandemic, neighbours must come together to help one another and stay connected. One can drop off groceries for an elderly neighbour. One can also interact with friends through phone and video calls.

Be friendly with neighbours

Apply it!

How did you spend your time during the pandemic lockdown? Did you interact with your neighbours?

landmarks: buildings that you can see clearly from a distance and that will help you to know where you are

Skill Builder

21ST CENTURY SKILLS

Critical thinking skills:

1. Why should we help our neighbours?
2. How does a pharmacy help us?
3. What is an ATM?

Life skills: Rahul's neighbourhood friend Sajal has broken his leg. He cannot move for two weeks. List three ways in which Rahul can help and cheer up Sajal.

Communicative skills: Interview your neighbourhood vegetable seller. Ask:

1. For how many years have you been selling vegetables?
2. Which vegetable is the most popular?
3. How many people visit the shop daily?

Connect

Plant trees in your neighbourhood and encourage your friends to maintain cleanliness.

Wind up

- A neighbourhood has many places.
- Landmarks are buildings that make finding our house easy.
- We should keep our neighbourhood clean.

Exercises

A. Choose the correct option to fill in the blanks.

1. We should .... our neighbours.

   a. not help b. help c. not talk to

2. .... is the place where we keep money and costly things.

   a. Fire station b. Bank c. Hotel

3. We should not .... in and around our neighbourhood.

   a. throw waste b. clean c. plant trees

4. .... is a place where one can fuel up their vehicles.

   a. Petrol pump b. Bank c. Market

B. Quiz time!! Answer this quiz about your neighbourhood.

1. Name two places you cross in your neighbourhood while going to the school.
2. What is the name of the street where you live?
3. Name the metro station/bus stop located in or near your neighbourhood.
4. Name the shop nearest to your house.
5. Which is your favourite place in your neighbourhood?

C. Answer in one word.

1. What makes our lives comfortable in a neighbourhood? ....
2. What helps us to locate places easily? ....
3. How should we act with our neighbours? ....

Think Big — English Fun

Mr. and Mrs. Paul have just shifted to your neighbourhood. Help them identify the different places and fill in the blanks.

1. Mrs. Paul wants to make a salad. She will have to go to the .... to buy fresh vegetables.

   a. school b. greengrocer c. bakery

2. Mrs. Paul had bought new jewellery yesterday. Today she will have to go the .... to keep it safe.

   a. airport b. hospital c. bank

3. Mr. and Mrs. Paul are going to visit their cousin by bus. They should board it from the ....

   a. market b. bus stop c. school

4. Mrs. Paul wants to buy a dress for her daughter. She should go to the .... in her neighbourhood.

   a. shopping mall b. hospital c. bakery

5. Mr. Paul's car is out of fuel. He should go to the .... to refill it.

   a. petrol pump b. airport c. pharmacy

Learning Tools

Trace the path to help the car reach home. Name any two landmarks that you see.

Web links:

https://kids.nationalgeographic.com/nature/article/clean-it-up

Last accessed on 30 August 2021

6. Directions and Time

Warm up

Sing and act out this song with your friends.

You put your right foot in.
You take your right foot out.
You put your right foot in.
And you shake it all about.
You do the hokey pokey
And you turn yourself around
That's what it's all about!

We use the words left and right to explain the **position** of a place. We also talk about how far it is and if it is above or below something. But, this only works if the place that we are trying to locate is nearby.

What's in the picture?

Look at the picture and write the position of the three girls.

1. Ina is standing on the .... side of Tina.
2. Anya is standing on the .... side of Tina.
3. Tina is jumping .... Ina and Anya.

Directions

A direction is the path where someone or something moves or faces. Directions are words or pictures that show you how to get somewhere. When we look at big maps that show where places are, we use east, west, north and south to explain directions. These are the four main directions.

position: the place, situation or location of a person or thing

We can find out directions once we know where east is. East is the direction in which the Sun can be seen in the morning. East and west are **opposite** to each other. If you stand and face the east, then north would be on your left and south would be on your right. We can also use a compass to find out directions. A compass is an instrument with a needle that always points to the north.

Using a compass

A compass

Let us understand the directions by looking at a neighbourhood **sketch**.

You will see that the restaurant is to the east of the pharmacy. The bakery is to the west of the pet shop. The pharmacy is to the south of the bakery and the pet shop is to the north of the restaurant.

A neighbourhood sketch

Green Earth

We should water plants in the morning or in the evening because the water dries up quickly in the afternoon due to heat.

Time

We do different things at different times of the day. We can tell the difference between morning and afternoon by looking at the position of the Sun in the sky.

When the Sun appears, we know it is morning. When the Sun is high in the sky, we know it is afternoon and when the Sun goes down, we know it is evening.

We can look at our **shadow** to find out what time of the day it is. A shadow always forms on the opposite side of the light.

Morning Afternoon Evening

opposite: located at the end or other side of something; sketch: a rough drawing; shadow: a dark area or shape produced by a body coming between the rays of light and a surface

A clock or a watch is a device that gives us the exact time of the day. Its two hands—one long and one short—help us to tell the time. When we use a clock or a watch, time is measured in hours, minutes and seconds. There are 24 hours in a day.

When the long hand is at 12 and the short hand is at 3, it is 3 o'clock.

FACT CHECK

A calendar helps us to know the dates for all seven days of the week.

Apply it!

Write the time at which you do these activities.

1. At what time of the day do you eat breakfast? ....
2. At what time do you return from school? ....
3. When do you go out to play? ....
4. When do you wear your pyjamas? ....

Skill Builder

21ST CENTURY SKILLS

Critical thinking skills: Solve these riddles. Remember that a compass always points to the north.

1. If your compass points to your left, which direction is south? ....
2. If your compass points to your front, where is east? ....
3. If the hour hand is at 12 and the Sun is up, what time of the day will it be? ....

Life skills:

1. Who wakes you up for school?
2. What happens when you get up late in the morning and miss your bus? Who drops you to school?

Communicatives skill: Answer these questions.

1. My friend with whom I share my desk in class sits on my ______ (left/right) side.
2. The classroom door is on my ______ (left/right) side.
3. I write with my ______ (left/right) hand.

Information literacy: What do you understand by the term 'GPS'?

Connect

Look at a clock and learn to read the time. Be on time for all your daily activities.

Wind up

- East, west, north and south are the four main directions.
- A compass is an instrument used to find directions.
- We can tell time by looking at the Sun's position or at a clock or a watch.
- A day has 24 hours.

Exercises

A. Choose the correct option to fill in the blanks.

1. .... is opposite to west.
   a. North b. East c. South
2. A compass always points to the ....
   a. north b. east c. west
3. .... is opposite to north.
   a. East b. South c. West
4. If you are facing east, then north is on your ....
   a. left b. back c. right
5. A clock has .... hands.
   a. four b. two c. five

B. Draw the hour and minute hands in the clocks according to the time given below.

6:00

10:00

4:00

C. Answer in one word.

1. What do we call east, west, north and south collectively? ....
2. Which instrument helps us to find directions? ....
3. What tells us the exact time? ....

Think Big

Thinking skill

Imagine you are standing at the gate of a Wildlife Park. Follow the instructions and trace the path with red crayon. Tell where would you finally reach.

- Enter the gate and turn right.
- Walk towards the bear enclosure.
- Then turn left after crossing the lion enclosure.
- Walk straight towards the elephants, you would cross the flamingos.
- Turn left and walk straight.
- Your destination is on the left of the horse enclosure, in front of the hippopotamus!

  Where did you finally reach?

Learning Tools

Let's make a paper plate clock.

Material required: one white paper plate and one smaller coloured paper plate, a small set of numbers, glue, coloured pens, thin cardboard or foam, board pin

Method:

1. Take the big paper plate and glue the smaller coloured plate on it.
2. Paste the numbers from 1 to 12 onto the smaller plate or write down the numbers using coloured pens.
3. Ask an adult to write the minutes on the edges of the bigger plate.
4. Cut out the hands of the clock from a thin cardboard or foam with the help of an adult.
5. Fix them in the centre of the coloured plate using a board pin. These are your hour and minute hands.

Your clock is ready to show time as you want!

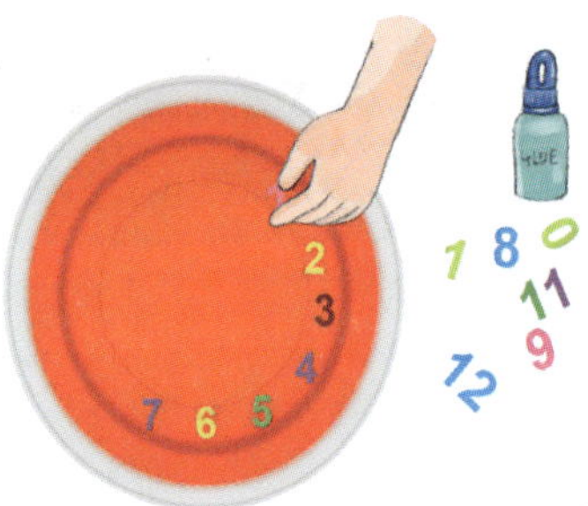

Web links:

https://kids.nationalgeographic.com/search?q=Time&location=srp&type=manual

https://spaceplace.nasa.gov/time-travel/en/

Last accessed on 30 August 2021

7. Food and Clothes

Warm up

Identify the two professions given in the picture.

....

We all need food to live. Food makes us healthy and strong. We drink milk and eat a variety of food like fruits, vegetables, grains, milk products and meat products.

Water is also an important part of food. It helps us to digest the food we eat.

Sources of Food

We get food items from various sources. Let us find out about them. Most of our food, such as fruits, vegetables, spices, oil, **beverages** and dry fruits, comes from plants and is grown by farmers.

Fruits

Cereals

Vegetables

Oils

We also get some food items from animals, such as milk, eggs and meat. We get butter, curd and cheese from milk.

Milk and milk products

Meat and fish

Eggs

beverage: a drink other than water

FACT CHECK

Green and leafy vegetables keep our bones and teeth strong.

What's in the picture?

Match the food item with its source.

Cooked and Uncooked Food

We eat food in different forms. Some food items can be eaten raw, without cooking. Vegetables like tomatoes, cucumber and carrots can be eaten raw. Fruits are also eaten raw. We cook some food items to make them soft and tasty. Pulses, cereals and meat are eaten in cooked form.

Good Food Habits

Some good and healthy habits are:

- We must eat healthy food and chew it properly. We should avoid eating junk food like burgers and fries.
- We must not waste our food.
- We must wash our hands before and after eating.
- We must drink plenty of water daily.

Apply it! E

Tick (✓) the food items that are eaten in their cooked form.

1. Eggs
2. Potatoes
3. Mangoes
4. Chicken
5. Rice
6. Curd

Clothes

Clothes protect our body from heat, rain, cold and the wind. We wear different types of clothes in different seasons. Cotton clothes are worn in the summer, while woollen clothes are worn in the winter season. We wear a raincoat and gumboots when it rains. We get cotton from the cotton plant and wool from the fur of the sheep.

Different clothes

Green Earth

In ancient times, people used dyes made from berries, flowers and plants to colour their clothes. Now also, natural dyes are used for clothes.

Types of Clothes

People wear different kinds of clothes for different activities. Swimsuits and swimming trunks are worn for swimming, pyjamas for sleeping and sportswear for exercise or for playing sports. **Astronauts** wear spacesuits when they go to space. **Ballerinas** wear tutus, divers wear diving suits and a cook wears an apron and a cap.

Clothes for different activities

Sometimes a group of people wear special clothes. These special clothes worn by people to work or to school are called uniforms.

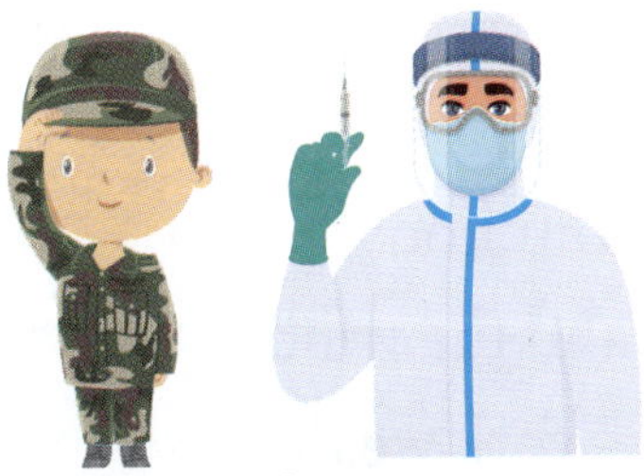

Uniforms

Students, nurses, doctors, soldiers, lawyers and police officers wear uniforms.

Sometimes people wear **traditional** clothes for festivals and weddings and costumes for dance or other performances.

Skill Builder

21ST CENTURY SKILLS

Critical thinking skills:

A. Using the words given in the help box, solve the crossword about the different clothes we wear.

Across
4. When it rains
5. When it is cold

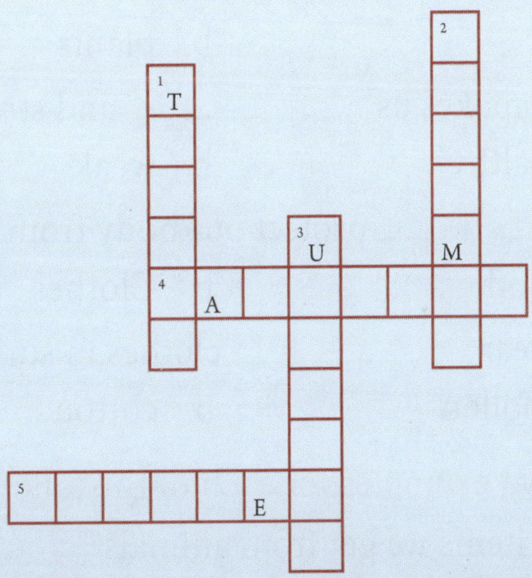

Down
1. When it is sunny and warm
2. When we go to bed
3. When we go to school

B. Why should we always keep food covered?

Life Skills: Tick (✓) the good activities that you do:

1. Always eat with your mouth closed. ☐
2. Start eating even before every one has been served. ☐
3. Play with the cutlery while waiting for the food. ☐
4. Take only as much food as you can eat and not waste. ☐

astronaut: a person who is trained for travelling in a spacecraft; ballerina: a woman ballet dancer; traditional: existed for a long time

Connect

Some people do not eat any meat and animal products such as milk, butter, cheese and curd. They are called vegans.

Wind up

- We need food and water to live, grow and stay healthy.
- We get food from plants and animals.
- Food gives us energy, protects us from diseases and builds our body.
- We wear clothes to protect our body from heat, rain, cold and the wind.
- We wear clothes according to the season, occasion and the work we do.

Exercises

A. Choose the correct option and fill in the blanks.

1. We get food from .... and animals.
   a. air   b. plants   c. water
2. Food makes us .... and strong.
   a. healthy   b. weak   c. sleepy
3. .... protect our body from heat, rain, cold and the wind.
   a. Food   b. Clothes   c. Air
4. We wear .... clothes in summers.
   a. woollen   b. cotton   c. rubber

B. Write two examples for each of the following.

1. Food items we get from animals ....
2. People who wear uniforms ....
3. Food items eaten cooked ....
4. Food items eaten raw ....
5. Clothes worn in winters ....

C. Answer in one word.

1. What should we drink daily? ....
2. Should we eat vegetables and fruits? ....
3. What do astronauts wear when they go to space? ....
4. What do ballerinas wear? ....

Think Big

Number Fun

Look at the numbers given to each hat. Solve the equations and write the correct answer.

Learning Tools

A. Let us make sprouts chaat.
Ingredients: 1 cup sprouts, 2 cups of chopped cucumber, tomato and onion mix, salt, pepper, chaat masala and 1 tablespoon lemon juice
Method:

1. Take the sprouts in a bowl.
2. Add chopped cucumber, onions and tomatoes.
3. Add salt, pepper and chaat masala and lemon juice this mixture.
4. Mix well. Your tangy sprouts chaat is ready.

B. Let us do vegetable printing.
Material required: A plain handkerchief, fabric paint and a potato
Method:

1. Ask an adult to cut out a star from a potato.
2. Dip the potato star design in the fabric paint and press it on the handkerchief. Let it dry. Your printed handkerchief is ready!

Web links:

https://kids.nationalgeographic.com/weird-but-true/article/morefood
https://easyscienceforkids.com/all-about-what-do-you-wear/
Last accessed on 30 August 2021

8. Water We Drink

Warm up

What do you see in the picture?
What would you do if you see this at home?

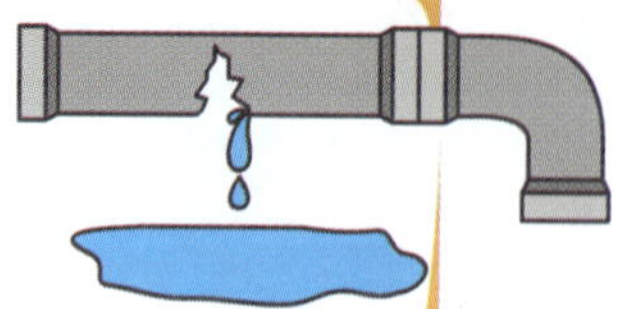

Need for Water

All living beings need water to live. Plants need water to make their food. Animals need water for drinking and bathing. We need water for drinking, washing clothes, cooking, bathing, cleaning, gardening, farming and for many other activities. We also need water to put out fire.

Drinking

Cooking

Watering plants

Putting out fire

Sources of Water

We get water in our homes from a tap. Do you know where does this water come from? Water comes down from the clouds in the form of rain and snow. Rain is the main **source** of water. Rainwater fills up the rivers, lakes, ponds and seas. These are natural sources of water.

> **FACT CHECK**
> Ice and snow form glaciers on high mountains.

River

Glacier

Sea

source: the point or place from which something originates

The water in the rivers, lakes, ponds and seas is called surface water. Canals and dams are human-made sources of water. They are built to store large quantities of surface water.

Some amount of rainwater seeps into the ground and gets collected as groundwater. We get groundwater through wells and hand pumps, usually for drinking and irrigating the field.

Handpump

Well

A dam

Thus, three main sources of water are rainwater, surface water and groundwater.

Storing Water

It is important for us to store water so that we can use it later. At home, we store water in bottles, jugs and buckets. Large quantities of water are stored in water tanks. We also build **dams** to store water.

Water bottle

Water tank

Saving Water

Water is important for us. We should save water and never waste it. There are many ways to save water.

Close the tap while brushing your teeth.

Pour leftover water into a plant instead of throwing it away.

Inform elders if a tap is leaking.

Apply it! E

List three ways in which you can help to save water.

What's in the picture?

What is happening here?

1. How would you practice this at home?
2. How can you use the collected rainwater?

dam: a human-made lake for storing water

Clean water

We should drink clean water. If we drink water that is dirty, we might fall sick. The containers where we store water should also be clean.

People throw waste and garbage into water bodies. This makes the water in lakes and ponds dirty and unfit for drinking. This should not be done. We should keep all sources of water clean.

Do not throw garbage into water bodies

Green Earth

Some rivers are so dirty that even fish cannot live in them.

Skill Builder

Critical thinking skills: What will happen if all the water on the Earth finishes?

Life skills: Tick (✓) the things that you should do.

1. Turn off the tap while brushing your teeth ☐
2. Play with water ☐
3. Drink water directly from the tap ☐

Information literacy: How do dams store water to make electricity? Find out which is the biggest dam in India.

Connect

The farmers in India use major part of freshwater for irrigation and use tube wells to extract groundwater.

Wind up

- Living beings need water to live.
- There are many uses of water.
- We should store and save water.
- We should always drink clean water.

Exercises

A. Choose the correct word from the box and name these uses of water.

bathing	swimming	cleaning	washing hands

....

B. Choose the correct option to fill in the blanks.

1. .... is a source of water.
   a. Pipe b. River c. Glass
2. Water for drinking can be stored in .... and ....
   a. plate and spoon b. pond and lake c. bottles and jugs
3. .... is an activity that cannot be done without water.
   a. Swimming b. Sleeping c. Dancing
4. If we drink .... water, we might fall sick.
   a. coloured b. dirty c. clean
5. .... are built to store large quantities of water.
   a. Bottles b. Dams c. Jugs

C. Answer in one word.

1. Name one use of water. ....
2. Name one source of water. ....
3. What makes the water in lakes and ponds dirty? ....
4. Should we drink dirty or clean water? ....

Think Big

English Fun

Read the sentences. Tick (✓) the correct actions that help save water.

1. I turn off the water tap after use

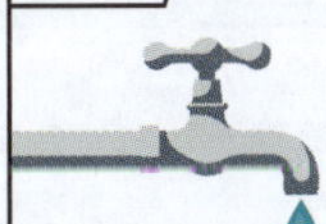

2. I use a watering can to water plants

3.

I give my pet

clean water | to drink

4.

I use

a hose | to wash my car

5.

I collect

rainwater | to reuse later

6.

I throw

garbage | in the river

Learning Tools

Find the names of atleast seven sources of water in the word search.

Handpump
Lake
Pond
Rain
River
Sea
Spring
Well

Z	R	A	I	N	B	O	Q	A
H	A	N	D	P	U	M	P	K
Q	Y	X	V	K	O	O	Q	R
U	A	S	S	Y	A	J	C	I
F	L	P	N	E	D	P	O	V
Q	A	R	Y	V	A	O	X	E
S	K	I	F	K	W	N	V	R
E	E	N	O	D	C	D	G	I
A	J	G	A	W	E	L	L	L

Web links:

https://climatekids.nasa.gov/10-things-water/
Last accessed on 30 August 2021

WORKSHEET

Worksheet (Chapters 5-8)

A. Choose the correct option to fill in the blanks.

1. Important buildings that are close to our house are called ....

   a. directions   b. landmarks   c. market

2. There are .... hours in a day.

   a. 24   b. 18   c. 21

3. The direction opposite to the south is ....

   a. west   b. east   c. north

4. We get some food items from .... such as milk, eggs and meat.

   a. plants   b. animals   c. sea

5. .... are special clothes worn by people to work or to school.

   a. Tutus   b. Raincoat   c. Uniforms

6. Rain, oceans, sea, rivers, pond, stream and wells are various .... of water.

   a. forms   b. places   c. sources

B. Write T for True and F for False.

1. We must wash our hands before and after eating food. ☐
2. A compass is used to tell the time. ☐
3. The Sun sets in the west. ☐
4. We keep money and costly things in an ATM. ☐
5. We need water for swimming and for putting out fires. ☐

C. Look at the pictures and write one sentence about it.

1. 

....

....

2. 

....

....

3. 

....

....

4. 

....

....

5. 

....

....

6. 

....

....

9. Air We Breathe

Warm up

Do you blow bubbles? Do you know how are they formed? Discuss how bubbles are formed.

Air is all around us. It moves from one place to another. It can be hot or cold.

Air has **speed**. This is why we feel the air when our hair starts blowing on a windy day.

Moving air is called wind. Wind blows in a **direction**. The plants sway in the direction of the wind.

When the wind is too strong, it becomes a storm. A storm can **uproot** trees.

Wind

Storm

Air has **weight**. We cannot see air but, it takes up space and has weight. When we blow air in a flat balloon, the balloon takes up space and becomes heavy.

FACT CHECK

A wind gauge measures the speed of the wind.
A wind vane tells us the direction of the wind.

speed: the rate at which someone or something moves; direction: the way in which someone or something moves; uproot: to pull a tree or a plant out of the ground; weight: how heavy something is

Apply it!

Let us do an activity on air. Take two flat balloons and one long wooden stick. Tie one flat balloon on one side of the stick. Fill the other balloon with air. Now, hang it on the other side of the stick. What do you see?

You will see that the stick tilts towards the blown-up balloon. If you hold both the balloons in your hands, you will feel that the balloon filled with air is heavier than the flat balloon. This is because air has weight.

Air Helps Us

Air is very useful for all of us. Air helps carry seeds of trees and plants to other places. Later, these seeds help in forming new plants.

Air helps carry seeds.

Air helps aeroplanes to fly.

Air is filled in a football.

Air helps to move the blades of windmills.

Air helps fire to burn.

Air helps to dry clothes.

Air helps sailboats to sail on water.

Air helps hot air balloons to rise and fly.

Air helps kites and paper aeroplanes to fly.

Clean Air

Clean and fresh air is **essential** for our good health. Air becomes dirty when dust, smoke and harmful gases are released from factories and vehicles. Burning of wood, paper and leaves make the air dirty. Cover your face while coughing or sneezing because the germs might make other people sick too and pollute the air.

Air pollution

Green Earth

Ask your parents not to use the car for short distances as this causes air pollution.

What's in the picture?

☐ ☐ ☐ ☐ ☐

Tick (✓) the musical instruments that we would blow in to produce sound.

Keeping Air Clean

We must take some steps to keep the air clean so that we may not fall sick.

- Ride your bicycle more, use the car less.
- Take the school bus to school or use carpooling to reduce pollution.
- Turn off the lights, fans, heaters and all other electrical appliances when you are not using them.
- Plant trees as they help clean the air.
- Ask your parents to get pollution checks done on their cars.

Kids cycling

essential: necessary

Skill Builder

Critical thinking skills:

1. Why can we not live on the moon?
2. Do cars that use electricity instead of petrol and diesel cause harm to the air?

Life skills: Tick (✓) what can be done to keep the air clean.

1. Burning leaves and crackers ☐
2. Planting trees ☐
3. Walking for short distances ☐
4. Sneezing and coughing without covering the mouth ☐

Connect

New Delhi, the capital of India, is one of the most polluted cities in the world.

Wind up

- Air has speed, direction and weight. It also applies force and takes up space.
- Air is useful to us in many ways.
- Smoke and dust makes air dirty.
- We should keep the air clean by planting trees and using a bicycle to travel for short distances.

Exercises

A. Choose the correct option from the box and fill in the blanks.

boats	smoke	wind gauge	clean

1. An instrument used for measuring wind speed is called a ....
2. .... makes the air dirty.
3. Air helps .... to sail on water.
4. We should keep the air .... by planting trees.

B. Tick (✓) the correct statements.

1. Air does not have force. ☐
2. Wind moves in one direction. ☐
3. Dirty air is healthy for the body. ☐

C. Answer the following.

1. What do we call moving air?
2. Write any two uses of air.
3. Write any two properties of air.

Think Big

Art integration

Make your own pinwheel!

Material required: Craft paper, scissors, glue stick, markers, a pencil with eraser and push pin

Method:

1. Cut out two identical squares from a craft paper.
2. Draw diagonal lines on them and decorate the squares.

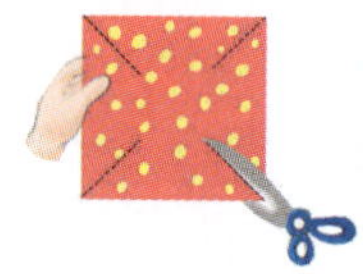

3. Apply glue on the squares and paste them together.
4. Once the glue dries, make a slit along the four diagonal dotted lines.

5. Take each of 8 alternate tips and glue to the center of the square without folding it.
6. Insert a push pin at the center to hold all four tips together.

7. Attach the pinwheel to a pencil by pushing the pin into the pencil's eraser. Blow it and watch it spin!!

Learning Tools

Look at the pictures and name the things that pollute the air. Suggest ways to reduce air pollution.

1.  ____________
2.  ____________
3.  ____________
4.  ____________

Web links:

https://climatekids.nasa.gov/air-pollution/

Last accessed on 30 August 2021

10. More About Plants

Warm up

Can you name the types of plants shown here?

_______________ _______________ _______________

Types of Plants

You know that there are different types of plants. All plants require sunshine, water and air to grow properly. Some plants grow on land, while some others grow in water. Some of the water plants are duckweed, lotus and water hyacinth.

Lotus

Water Hyacinth

Parts of a Plant

A plant has many parts. Each part of the plant performs an important function.

Roots grow under the ground and they **firmly** hold the plant in the soil. They also help draw up water and **nutrients** from the soil.

The stem grows above the ground. It provides support to the plant and carries food and water to all parts of the plant.

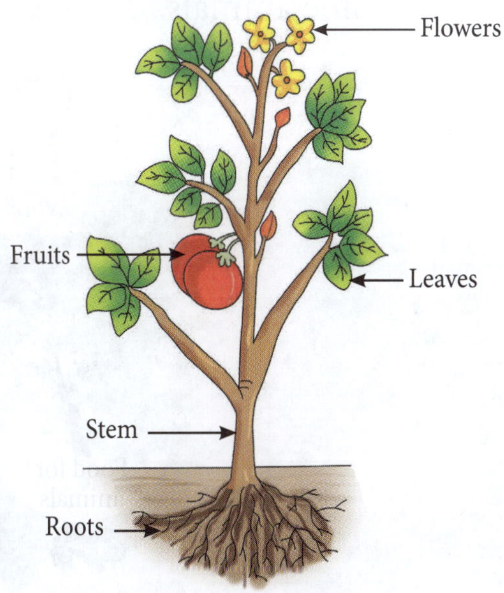

Parts of a plant

firmly: in a strong way; nutrients: any substance needed in order to live and grow

Leaves use water, sunlight and nutrients to make food for the plant. Green leaves make their own food. Flowers help to produce new plants. Some flowers become fruits. Fruits have seeds inside them. These seeds, when planted, grow into new plants.

Apply it!

Take three saplings and keep them under these conditions.
Sapling 1: Keep it closed in a shoe box and water it regularly.
Sapling 2: Keep it in an open area but do not water it.
Sapling 3: Keep it in an open area and water it regularly.
Observe them for two weeks. What do you notice?

FACT CHECK

Research indicates that one single family uses six trees worth of paper each year.

Uses of Plants

Plants provide us with:

- vegetables, fruits and cereals or food grains
- medicines and spices
- oils and perfumes
- wood for making furniture
- oxygen to breathe
- food and home for some animals

Green Earth

Do not throw or burn dry leaves and vegetable peels. Put them in a compost pit and turn the waste into manure for plants.

Things we get from plants

Taking Care of Plants

We should take care of the plants around us. We should water them regularly. We must never cut trees because trees make our planet look beautiful.

What's in the picture?

Colour the box green for the things we get from plants.

Connect

An average size tree can provide enough wood to make thousands of pencils.

Skill Builder

21ST CENTURY SKILLS

Critical thinking skills: What happens if we burn leaves and twigs? What should we do instead of this?

Communication skills: Discuss in class why the action shown in the picture is incorrect.

Life skills: Talk to the gardener of your neighbourhood park. Find out how he takes care of the plants.

Creativity and innovation skills:

Look at the picture. How can you help the bird which has lost its home?

Wind up

- A plant has many parts.
- Plants make their own food.
- Plants need air, water and sunlight to grow.
- Plants are useful to us.
- Plants make the air clean. We should take care of the plants around us.

Exercises

A. Choose the correct option to fill in the blanks.

1. The part of the plant that has seeds in it is called a ....

   a. root b. leaf c. fruit

2. .... is the part of a plant that is found in the soil.

   a. Stem b. Root c. Branch

3. The .... carries food and water to all parts of a plant.

   a. leaf b. bud c. stem

4. Plants provide us with ....

   a. oils and perfumes b. milk and cheese c. silk and plastic

5. Plants help to make the air ....

   a. clean b. dirty c. rise

B. Look at the picture and label the different parts of the plant.

C. Answer the following.

1. Name any two water plants.
2. Name any two parts of a plant.
3. Name one way in which we can take care of plants.

Think Big

Craft fun

Let us make a tree using foil.

Material required: foil, chart paper, and green, yellow and brown paints

Method:

1. Take a white chart paper. Ask an adult to help you make the trunk of a big tree with brown paint.
2. Keep yellow and green paint in a dish.
3. Dip a ball of crumpled foil in the dish with paints and place it above the trunk to make leaves and flower.
4. Repeat this step as many times as you like to make your tree big and pretty.

Learning Tools

Look at the two columns and place the given words in their correct columns.

sunlight flower leaves air roots soil fruits stem water

Requirements of a plant	Parts of a plant

Web links:

https://www.nationalgeographic.org/education/resource-library/?q=plants&page=1&per_page=25

https://www.dkfindout.com/uk/search/plants/

Last accessed on 30 August 2021

11. More About Animals

Warm up

How can you help to take care of pet animals?

Animals are found everywhere—some live on land, some live in water and some live both on land and in water. The natural environment in which an animal normally lives is called its habitat.

Animal Habitats

Animals like tigers, giraffes, elephants, deer, lions, zebras, dogs and horses live on land.

Animals like monkeys, squirrels, birds and insects live on trees.

Animals like snakes and rats dig holes and tunnels under the ground to live. Rabbits make burrows to live. Animals like lions and bears live in **natural shelters** like a den or a cave.

Land animals

FACT CHECK

Animals living on land are called terrestrial animals and those living on trees are known as arboreal animals.

A rabbit lives in a burrow.

A lion lives in a cave.

natural: not made by humans but existing in nature ; shelter: place that is made to protect from bad weather or from danger

Sometimes, pets and farm animals live in shelters that humans make especially for them.

Cows live in a shed.

Dogs live in a kennel.

Hens live in a coop.

Horses live in a stable.

Animals like fish, dolphins and whales live in water. They are called aquatic animals. Sometimes, people keep fish in their home in an aquarium. Animals like tortoises, frogs and crocodiles can live on land as well as in water.

Aquatic animals

What's in the picture?

Name the animals that make trees their habitat.

....

....

....

....

....

....

....

How Animals Move

Animals walk, hop, crawl, fly and swim to move from one place to another.

Snails crawl

Parrots fly

Kangaroos hop

Fish swim

Apply it!

Write the names of three animals for each habitat.

1. Land ....
2. Water ....
3. Trees ....
4. Land and water ....

Animals Help Us

Animals help us in many ways. They give us milk, honey, meat, eggs and wool.

Cow gives us milk.

Bees give us honey.

Green Earth

Earthworms help the farmers to keep our land fertile.

Hen gives us eggs.

Sheep gives us wool.

Looking After Animals

Pets are animals that we keep at home. They are part of our family. We must take care of farm animals too and take them to a vet if they are unwell. Just like we love and care for our family members, we should love and care for our pet or farm animals also.

Caring for animals

Skill Builder

21ST CENTURY SKILLS

Critical thinking skills: Solve these riddles.

1. I met a creature on the road.
   On its back it had a load.
   It wasn't a mule and it wasn't a cow,
   Though two horns grew on its brow.

   ....

2. You can see me at the zoo.
   I've got four legs,
   But jump on two.
   I've got a little kid,
   And a big bag, too.

   ....

Life skills: Take some sugar and keep it in your balcony or in the garden. Wait for the ants to come and follow them to find out where they live. Record your observations.

1. Place where I kept the sugar crystals: ....
2. Time the ants took to reach the sugar crystals: ....
3. Place where they took the sugar crystals to: ....

Communication skills: If all the forests are destroyed, where will the animals and birds go? Discuss in class.

Connect

Many endangered animals in India, such as the Royal Bengal Tiger, Asian Elephant, Ganga Dolphin and Red Panda are reducing in number.

Wind up

- Animals live on land, trees and in water.
- Animals live in natural shelters, human-made shelters, in water or under the ground.
- Animals walk, hop, crawl, fly and swim to move from one place to the other.
- We must take care of our pet and farm animals.

Exercises

A. Choose the correct option to fill in the blanks.

1. A .... moves by crawling on the ground.
   a. snail b. fish c. squirrel
2. I can keep a .... as my pet animal.
   a. cat b. lion c. bee

3. I can't keep tigers and crocodiles at my home because they are .... animals.

   a. wild   b. domestic   c. pet

4. I should give .... to a goat to eat.

   a. chips   b. grass   c. fish

B. Match the columns.

	Column A		Column B
1.	Lives on trees	a.	Snake
2.	Lives in a coop	b.	Monkey
3.	Lives in water	c.	Hen
4.	Lives under the ground	d.	Frog
5.	Lives on both land and water	e.	Dolphin

C. Answer in one word.

1. Where do aquatic animals live? ....
2. Do all animals move in the same way? ....
3. What do pet animals require? ....

D. Read the names of few animals. List them according to their habitat.

Koala kangaroo dolphin shark tiger whale monkey horse squirrel

Terrestrial animals	Aquatic animals	Arboreal animals
____________	____________	____________
____________	____________	____________
____________	____________	____________

Think Big

English Fun

Read the sentences and tick (✓) the correct ones.

1. We get  from hen ☐

2. We get  from rabbit ☐

3. We get  from monkey

4. We get 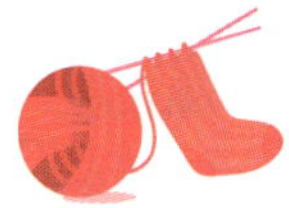 from sheep

5. We get  from bees

6. We get  from cows

Learning Tools

A. Let us make a tiger!

Material required: Paper cups, glue, orange paint, black marker pen, orange wool or thread

Method:

1. Paint the paper cup in orange, leaving a round white patch in the middle of the cup.
2. Using the black marker, draw stripes on the tiger. Add the eyes and nose as well.
3. Cut orange-coloured wool or string into two small pieces and glue it on top of the cup for the ears.
4. Use the remaining piece of string to make the tail.

The cup-o-tiger is ready!

B. Help the whale reach its baby.

Web links:

https://kids.nationalgeographic.com/nature/habitats
https://www.worldwildlife.org/habitats

Last accessed on 30 August 2021

12. Transport and Communication

Warm up

1. Identify this mode of transport used in many cities in India.
2. Have you travelled in it? Which stations did you cross?
3. What part of the travel did you like the most?

Transport

We use different means of transport to move from one place to another. We travel by road, rail, water and air using different vehicles.

Road Transport

Road transport

Earlier, people used animals, like camels, horses and elephants, to travel to faraway places. When the wheel was **invented**, travelling became easier.

Some common vehicles that we see on the road are cars, scooters, buses, trucks and bicycles. We also see some special vehicles on the roads like police car, fire engine and a hospital ambulance.

Green Earth

Vehicles that use petrol and diesel let out smoke into the air. Do you think that is good for the environment?

Fire engine

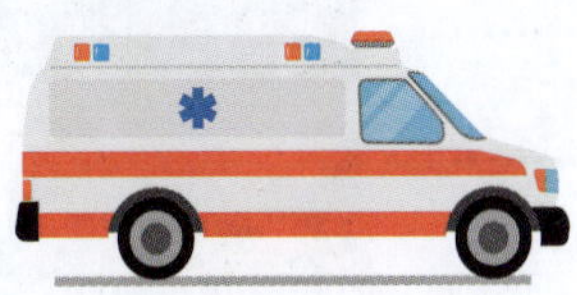

Ambulance

invented: to make something that has never been made before

Rail Transport

Railway station

We use trains to travel long distances and to carry goods.

Trains **ply** on railway tracks. A railway track has **rails** permanently built on the ground. Nowadays, metro and monorail are used in big cities.

Water Transport

Water transport

Water transport refers to the type of transport that moves on water. Ships, boats, steamers, yachts and sailboats are some means of water transport.

Air Transport

Aeroplanes, helicopters and gliders are some types of air transport. Aeroplanes and helicopters are very fast. Hot air balloons and cable cars also move in the air.

Aeroplane

Helicopter

Hot air balloon

What's in the picture?

Identify any five means of transport in the picture.

....

....

....

....

....

ply: to travel regularly along a particular way; rails: each of the two metal bars that form the track

Road Safety

We should always ensure safety when we are on the road. We must follow the traffic lights. Some rules for road safety are:

> **FACT CHECK**
>
> The Wright brothers invented and flew the first engine aeroplane.

- Always cross the road using a zebra crossing and with an elder.
- Always wear a seat belt in a car and helmet on a scooter or motorbike.
- Always walk on the footpath.
- Never get down from a moving vehicle.
- Never play on the road.

Always cross the road on a zebra crossing

Communication

Traffic police officer using hand gesture to direct traffic

We communicate with each other by speaking or writing. We also communicate using signs and symbols. A traffic police officer uses hand gestures to ask people to move in a particular direction or to stop.

Always wear a seat belt

Means of communication are the different ways that we use to communicate with others. Letters, emails, telephones and mobile phones are some ways in which we communicate with others.

Letter

Newspaper

Television

Mobile phone

Radio, newspapers, television and films are ways to communicate with many people at the same time.

Apply it!

Do we write, speak or use signs when we use these means of communication? Name the means and say how you use it to communicate with others.

Skill Builder

Critical thinking skills: Solve these riddles and identify the vehicle.

1. You need to wear a helmet. I move on two wheels. ....
2. You need to wear a seatbelt. I have four wheels. ....
3. I move on a track and I am very long. ....
4. 'Aye, aye,' says my captain as he steers me. ....

Life skills: Tick (✓) the correct answer.

1. Amit is working in Mumbai. He has to go to Delhi immediately. Which means of transport should he use?
   a. Car b. Ship c. Aeroplane
2. Roshni wants to go to Maldives islands. Which means of transport would she use?
   a. Ship b. Bus c. Train
3. You want to invite your friend to your birthday party. Which means of communication will you use?
   a. Write in a newspaper b. Call on the phone
4. How can one inform people about a storm?
   a. Through television b. Through email

Connect

In the coming years, there would be more electric vehicles that would run on roads. They would not pollute the environment.

Wind up

- We use different modes of transport to move from one place to another.
- Car, scooter, bicycle, auto rickshaw, bus and truck are the means of road transport.
- Ship, boat and yacht are the means of water transport.
- Aeroplane, helicopter and gliders are the means of air transport.
- We communicate by speaking, writing and by using signs and symbols.
- Letters, phones, newspapers, television are some means of communication.

Exercises

A. Write T for True and F for False.

1. We cannot communicate by using signs and symbols. ☐
2. Helicopters are a means of air transport. ☐
3. Hot air balloons travel on land. ☐
4. We can communicate by writing letters. ☐
5. A fire engine runs on wheels. ☐

B. Answer in one word.

1. Name any one special vehicle. ....
2. What do trains ply on? ....
3. A means of communication which helps to communicate with many people at the same time. ....

C. Look at the pictures and tick (✓) the correct action for road safety.

1.  ☐

2.  ☐

3. 

☐

4.  ☐

5.  ☐

6. 

☐

Think Big

English fun

You would have attended online school classes. Let us know more about it.

1. Who helped you to attend the online classes at home?
2. How was it different from going to your school?
3. Did you miss meeting your friends in school?

Learning Tools

Solve the crossword on the different means of transport. Name any two special vehicles that you see here.

Web links:

https://www.dkfindout.com/uk/animals-and-nature/insects/how-do-ants-communicate/
Last accessed on 30 August 2021

WORKSHEET

Worksheet (Chapters 9-12)

A. Choose the correct option to fill in the blanks.

1. Air takes up .... and has weight.

   a. form b. space c. colour

2. Some animals like .... can live on land as well as in water.

   a. crocodile b. fish c. tiger

3. We can communicate with each other by speaking, writing or using signs and ....

   a. symbols b. air c. notes

4. .... pollutes the air.

   a. Smoke b. Water c. Perfume

5. We should always cross the road using the ....

   a. line crossing b. red crossing c. zebra crossing

6. .... prepares food for the plant.

   a. Flower b. Leaf c. Stem

B. Match the columns.

	Column A		Column B
1.	Air helps these to rise	a.	Spices
2.	Buses and cars move on	b.	Ambulance
3.	A special vehicle	c.	Koala bear
4.	Animal that lives on trees	d.	Hot air balloon
5.	Plants provide us with	e.	Television
6.	A means of mass communication	f.	Wheels

C. Match the pictures of the food items to their source. One has been done for you.

1. 
Honey

2. 
Bread

3. 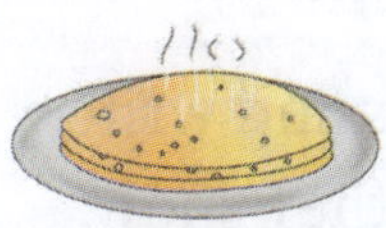
Chapati

4. 
Cheese

5. 
Butter

6. 
Fruits and vegetables

7. 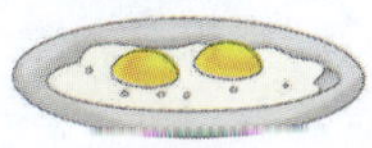
Eggs

8. 
Rice

9. 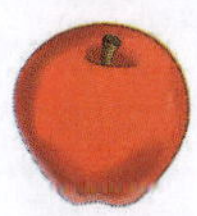
Apple

Plants Animals

13. Weather and Seasons

Warm up

- What kind of weather is being shown in the picture?
- What do you think these children are drinking?
- What do you like to drink after playing outside?

Weather

Windy

Weather changes every day. It can be sunny, foggy, rainy, **cloudy** or windy. Weather can also change many times in a day.

When there is a lot of wind, the weather is windy.

When it is sunny outside, the Sun is up and the weather is warm to hot.

Rainy

Weather is foggy when there is a low cloud, which makes it difficult for us to see things.

On rainy days, there is thunder and lightning in the sky. We use raincoats, umbrellas and gumboots.

On cloudy days, the sky is covered with clouds.

What's in the picture?

Look at these icons and write which weather do they show.

1. ....
2. ....
3. ....
4. ....

cloudy: when there are lots of clouds in the sky

Seasons

Sometimes, the weather stays the same for a long period of time. We call it season. Every season lasts for around two to three months. Some seasons are hot and some are cold.

India has five main seasons. They are spring, summer, monsoon, autumn and winter. People dress according to the season.

Spring

Spring

In spring, the days are pleasant. Plants grow new leaves in this season. Flowers bloom the most in spring.

Summer

Summer

Summer is the hottest season. The Sun shines the brightest and the wind is dry and hot. We use coolers, fans and air conditioners to keep ourselves cool. To stay cool in the heat, we wear light cotton clothes. We must drink plenty of water during summer. We should not play outside when the Sun is too hot in the summers.

Monsoon

Monsoon

In the monsoon season, it rains a lot. We wear raincoats and **gumboots**, and carry umbrellas to keep us dry. We must avoid playing outside when it rains.

Sometimes, it rains so much in some places that these places get **flooded** with water.

Autumn

Autumn

Autumn is a very short season that comes after the monsoon. It is neither too hot nor too cold during this time. Trees **shed** their leaves in this season.

Green Earth

We should collect rainwater and use it later.

flooded: a large amount of water covering an area of land which is usually dry; shed: to lose; gumboots: shoes worn during the rainy season

Winter

Winter is the coldest season of the year. During this season, cold and chilly winds blow and there is snowfall in some places. We wear woollen clothes and sweaters to keep ourselves warm. Heaters and fireplaces keep us warm during the winter months.

Winter

Apply it!

Write the months in which these seasons occur in India.

1. Summer ....
2. Monsoon ....
3. Autumn ....
4. Winter ....
5. Spring ....

FACT CHECK

Antarctica has six months of daylight in its summer and six months of darkness in its winter.

Skill Builder

Critical thinking skills:

1. Why should you not stay out in the Sun for too long?
2. Why is rain important to the farmers?
3. Why do we wear sweaters in winters?

Life skills: Tick (✓) the things that tell us what we should do during the summer season.

1. Drink lots of water	☐	3. Eat an ice cream	☐
2. Sit by a heater	☐	4. Drink hot soup	☐

Connect

Animals like bears and squirrels sleep throughout the winter season.

Wind up

- Weather changes every day. It can be sunny, foggy, rainy, cloudy or windy.
- When the weather remains the same for a long period, it is called a season.
- In India, we have five seasons—spring, summer, monsoon, autumn and winter.

Exercises

A. Unscramble the words and name the seasons.

1. AMUNUT ....
2. SMMURE ....
3. MOOONNS ....
4. SIGNPR ....
5. WTRINE ....

B. Choose the correct option to fill in the blanks.

1. .... is the hottest time of the year.

   a. Summer   b. Spring   c. Winter

2. Leaves fall during the .... season.

   a. winter   b. summer   c. autumn

3. We wear woollen clothes during the .... season.

   a. summer   b. winter   c. monsoon

4. .... is the wettest season of the year.

   a. Monsoon   b. Winter   c. Autumn

C. Answer in one word.

1. What do we wear to keep ourselves dry from the rain? ....
2. What do we like to do during the summer months? ....
3. What keeps us warm during winters? ....

Think Big

Number Fun

Look at the equations and answer the questions. One has been done for you.

1.  9 – 5 = 4

2.  .... = ?

3.  .... = ?

4.  .... = ?

5.  .... = ?

Learning Tools

Which clothes are worn in which seasons? Write their numbers in the blanks. One has been done for you.

Web links:

https://www.jpl.nasa.gov/edu/learn/slideshow/the-change-of-seasons-views-from-space/

Last accessed on 30 August 2021

14. Celebration Time

Warm up

1. In which festival are these objects used?

   .... and ....

2. Which is your favourite festival?

   ....

In India, we celebrate different types of festivals—religious, harvest and national festivals.

Religious Festivals

Let us learn about some religious festivals of India.

Holi is known as the 'festival of colours'. People apply colours to one another.

Dussehra celebrates the victory of good over evil.

Janmashtami is a festival that celebrates the birthday of Lord Krishna.

Gautama Buddha's birthday is celebrated as Buddha Purnima.

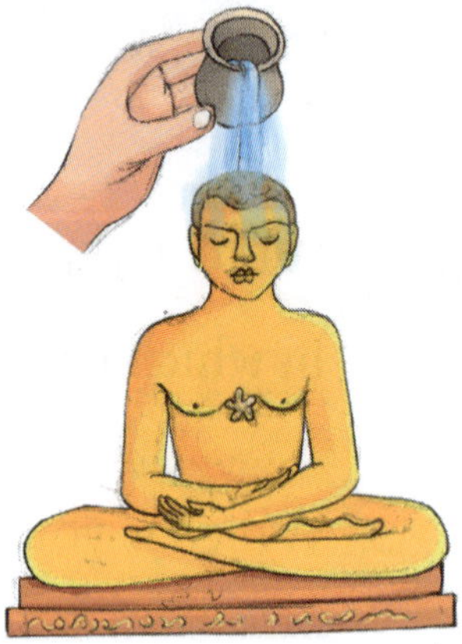

Guru Nanak Jayanti celebrates Guru Nanak's birthday. People eat at **langar** and sing **kirtan**.

People celebrate Mahavir Jayanti on the birthday of Mahavira.

Navroze marks the beginning of the Parsi new year.

Green Earth

During Holi, we should use organic and natural colours as they do not harm either our skin or the environment.

FACT CHECK

Pandit Nehru's birthday is celebrated as Children's Day on 14th November and Dr. Radhakrishnan's birthday as Teachers' Day on 5th September.

National Festivals

There are some festivals that are celebrated by every Indian. These are called national festivals.

Independence Day is celebrated on 15th August every year. On this day, the Prime Minister of India hoists the national flag at the Red Fort in Delhi.

Independence Day

langar: a practice run by Sikhs, where people can eat free meals; kirtan: devotional singing

Gandhi Jayanti

Gandhi Jayanti is celebrated on 2nd October to celebrate Mahatma Gandhi's birthday. He is known as the 'Father of our nation'.

India celebrates Republic Day on 26th January every year by conducting a colourful parade at Rajpath in Delhi.

Republic Day

Harvest Festivals

Harvest festivals are celebrated when farmers **harvest** their crops during the year. Many harvest festivals are celebrated in India.

Makar Sankranti is celebrated by flying kites. People also take a dip in **holy** rivers on this day.

Makar Sankranti

What's in the picture?

Look at these students dressed to celebrate an Indian festival.

1. Which festival do you think they are celebrating?
2. How do you celebrate the same festival in your school?

Onam is celebrated in Kerala with boat races, rangoli and feasts.

Onam

harvest: to cut and gather crops; holy: connected with god or religion

Bihu

Pongal is celebrated in Tamil Nadu with dishes made of harvested rice.

Bihu is celebrated in Assam with dances and feasts.

Pongal

Lohri is celebrated in Punjab with dances around a bonfire.

Lohri

Apply it!

Find out which parts of India celebrate New Year in April. What are these festivals called?

Skill Builder

Critical thinking skills: Do you think that dipping huge statues of deities in a river is good for the river?

Life Skills: Earth Day is celebrated on 22nd April every year. People work towards saving the environment on this day. How would you celebrate Earth Day?

Connect

New Year's Day is celebrated in all countries every year.

Wind up

- We celebrate different kinds of festivals in India—religious, national and harvest.
- We eat special food, sweets and exchange gifts on these festivals.
- We should celebrate festivals with our friends and family.

Exercises

A. Name any two of the following festivals.

1. Festivals that we celebrate to mark somebody's birthday.

   ....

2. Festivals that we celebrate when crops are harvested.

   ....

3. Festivals that entire India celebrates.

   ....

B. Choose the correct option to fill in the blanks.

1. .... is celebrated in Kerala with boat race, rangoli and feasts.
   a. Dussehra b. Onam c. Lohri
2. .... is celebrated on Mahatma Gandhi's birthday.
   a. Gandhi Jayanti b. Bihu c. Holi
3. On .... Day, we conduct a colourful parade at Rajpath.
   a. Independence b. Pongal c. Republic
4. .... festival is celebrated by flying kites.
   a. Mahavir Jayanti b. Makar Sankranti c. Holi

C. Answer in one word.

1. Which festival is celebrated in Assam?
2. Which festival celebrates the victory of good over evil?
3. When do we celebrate Republic Day?
4. Which festival is known as the 'festival of colours'?

D. Colour the rangoli.

Think Big

Data Fun

Talk to ten students in your class. Ask them which part of the celebrations do they enjoy the most. Present your answer as a smiling face in the given pictograph. One has been done for you.

1. Spending time with family	☺
2. Meeting relatives	
3. Decorating your home	
4. Wearing new clothes	
5. Eating sweets	
6. Exchanging gifts	

Learning Tools

A. Find the names of at least seven festivals in the word grid.

K	J	P	O	N	G	A	L	H	R	A	F	T	M
M	L	A	A	C	Z	U	I	M	M	S	T	K	U
V	A	M	N	D	U	S	S	E	H	R	A	C	Q
W	A	H	Y	M	N	O	N	P	Y	U	A	S	O
G	U	R	P	U	R	A	B	L	U	R	Z	T	N
K	O	W	D	V	U	S	C	V	H	R	E	G	A
Y	T	U	P	B	I	H	U	E	I	A	A	L	M
L	H	P	H	L	R	R	S	T	A	L	P	B	Q
M	A	H	A	V	I	R	J	A	Y	A	N	T	I
J	A	N	A	M	A	S	H	T	A	M	I	S	L
B	U	D	H	P	U	R	N	I	M	A	I	Q	O
X	F	C	Z	K	F	B	I	H	U	A	H	G	D
M	A	K	A	R	S	A	N	K	R	A	N	T	I
M	E	J	V	U	S	H	W	E	T	Q	B	T	I
H	O	L	I	O	N	A	V	R	O	Z	E	V	I

HOLI
PONGAL
ONAM
BIHU
DUSSEHRA
GURPURAB
MAKARSANKRANTI
JANMASHTAMI
NAVROZE
BUDHPURNIMA
MAHAVIRJAYANTI

B. Lighting a diya is a common tradition in most festivals of India. Let's make a paper diya.

Material required: sheet of craft paper, crayons, scissors, glue and pencil

Method:

1. Take a sheet of craft paper and fold it like a fan.
2. Hold the folded paper from the center and turn it into a half circle. Paste the ends.
3. Draw a thin triangle shape and cut it out to make the flame.
4. Colour it and paste it in the center of the diya.
5. Decorate your diyas with glitter and stars. You can gift them to your friends.

Web links:

https://www.un.org/en/observances/international-days-and-weeks
https://www.india.gov.in/india-glance/culture-heritage

Last accessed on 30 August 2021

15. Our Earth

Warm up

Which means of transport would you use to go to this place?

The Earth is our home. It is a planet. It is shaped like an orange and is flattened at the top. The Earth moves around the Sun. It gets warmth and light from the Sun. The Earth is made up of land and water.

Landforms

Land is not the same everywhere. There are hills, mountains, valleys, deserts, plains and islands on Earth. These are called landforms.

Hills

Hills are areas of land that are higher than the surrounding land. They are usually rocky. A hill appears like a cone made on Earth.

Mountains are much higher than the hills. They often have rocks or snow at the top. Some mountains are fully covered with snow. They are cold at the top and get warmer as you go down.

Mountains

Valley

A valley is an area of lowland lying between two hills or mountains, often with a river running through it.

A plain is a flat area of land. Most of the people in the world live on the plains as the land is flat, easier to build on and to transport goods. Crops are also grown here. The weather is usually hot in such regions.

Plains

A plateau is a large, flat area of land, which is higher than the land around it. It is flat, like a table top.

Plateau

Desert

A desert is a dry area covered with sand. Deserts have many small hills of sand called sand dunes. There are very few plants, animals and humans in the desert areas.

An island is an area of land that is surrounded by water on all sides. Islands are found in oceans and seas.

Island

Water

Water covers three-fourth of the Earth's surface hence Earth is also called the 'blue planet'. We find water on Earth in the form of rain, oceans, seas, rivers, lakes and ponds.

Rivers are formed when the snow melts from high mountains.

River

Apply it!

1. Which type of landform is found in your city or town?

   ....

2. Which is the nearest water body in your city or town?

   ....

Green Earth

Our planet Earth gives us land and water. We must keep them both clean.

Taking care of Planet Earth

Earth gives us everything that we need. It gives us water, air, food, sunlight and many other things. We should take care of the planet and not dirty it. If Earth becomes too dirty, it will not be **liveable**. Since this is our home, we should keep it clean.

FACT CHECK

Rainwater is the cleanest form of water.

What's in the picture?

Observe the picture and answer the questions.

1. Can you identify the landform?
2. What are the people doing?
3. Why do you think they are doing this?

Skill Builder

21ST CENTURY SKILLS

Critical thinking skills: Why is the Sun important to us?

Information literacy:

1. Which is the longest river in India?
2. Which is the highest mountain in India?

Life skills: How can you help to take care of planet Earth? Tick (✓) the right answer.

1. Leave trash in the picnic area. ☐
2. Keep taps running and waste water. ☐
3. Plant a tree and look after it. ☐
4. Use plastic bags instead of cloth bags for shopping. ☐
5. Keep a bowl of water in the balcony for birds to drink. ☐

Connect

Water covers three parts of the Earth while land portion is only one part.

liveable: fit to live in

Wind up

- Earth is made up of land and water.
- Landforms found on Earth are hills, mountains, valleys, deserts, plains and islands.
- We find water on Earth in the form of oceans, seas, rivers, lakes and ponds.
- We should keep planet Earth clean.

Exercises

A. Choose the correct option to fill in the blanks.

1. .... is the cleanest form of water.

   a. Tapwater b. Rainwater c. Salt water

2. .... are formed when the snow melts from high mountains.

   a. Rivers b. Rain c. Wells

3. .... is a piece of land that is surrounded by water on all sides.

   a. An island b. A desert c. A valley

4. .... appears like a cone made on Earth.

   a. Valley b. Hills c. Plateau

B. Match the columns.

Column A	Column B
1. Most crops easily grow here	a. Earth
2. Landform where hills of sand are seen	b. Valley
3. Landform between mountains and hills	c. Plateau
4. Landform that looks like a table from the top	d. Plains
5. The blue planet	e. Desert

C. Answer in one word.

1. What are the small hills of sand in the desert called?
2. Which landform is covered with rocks or snow at the top?
3. What will happen if Earth becomes too dirty?

Think Big

Quiz time

A. Name two of each of these places located in India.

1. Mountains ....
2. Rivers ....
3. Beaches ....

B. Look at the picture and discuss two ways in which you can prevent it.

Learning Tools

Make your own study notes. Write one sentence about each of these landforms.

....
....

....
....

....
....

....
....

....
....

....
....

Web links:

https://spaceplace.nasa.gov/menu/earth/

Last accessed on 30 August 2021

16. Our Universe

Warm up

Look at the picture and answer the questions.

1. Which vehicle would we take to travel in space?
2. Which planet do you live in?
3. Which is bigger in size, the Sun or the moon?

The Earth is our home. It is one of the eight planets in the **universe**. These planets, along with the Sun and the moon make up one big family called the solar system. The Sun is at the centre of the solar system and all planets move around it.

Planet Earth

The Sun

The Sun appears first in the east direction in the morning and then sets in the evening. We see it in the sky in different positions at different times of the day.

The Sun is a star. It is a big ball of fire. It is very big in size but looks small to us because it is very far away. The Sun gives us light and heat. It also helps plants to grow. Sunlight is essential for our body.

The Sun

Green Earth

Sunlight is essential for the growth of plants and trees, without which we would not get clean air to breathe.

universe: the whole of space with the stars, the planets and the moons

The Planets

The eight planets of the solar system are Mercury, Venus, Earth, Mars, Jupiter, Saturn, Uranus and Neptune. Mercury is closest to the Sun and Neptune is **farthest** from the Sun. The planets get heat and light from the Sun. The Earth is the only planet on which life is possible because it has water and air.

The solar system

What's in the picture?

1. Can you identify which planet this is? ....
2. Like Earth is the third planet from the Sun, so how far is this planet from the Sun? ....
3. Is there life on this planet? ....

Moon

You can see the moon in the sky only at night. It moves around the Earth. The moon is smaller in size than the Earth and its surface is rocky. Its shape changes every night. When it appears in a full circle, it is called a full moon. But sometimes, only half of it is visible from the Earth. Sometimes, we don't even see the moon in the sky. This is called a new moon.

FACT CHECK

The first person to walk on the moon was an astronaut called Neil Armstrong.

Phases of moon

farthest: at the greatest distance

Stars

You see stars twinkling in the night sky. Stars have their own light. A group of stars that forms a pattern in the sky is called a constellation.

Stars Constellation

Apply it!

Observe the shape of the moon on the following days and draw it in the space given below. Does the shape of the moon change often?

My Observations

Day 1	Day 10	Day 14	Day 20	Day 28

Skill Builder

Critical thinking skills: Why is there life only on Earth and not on any other planet?

Information literacy: Which was the ninth planet, now called a dwarf planet?

Life skills: Observe the lengths of your shadow at different times of the day. At what time is your shadow the longest and at what time is it the shortest?

Connect

For years it was believed that Earth was the only planet in our solar system with liquid water.

Wind up

- Earth belongs to one big family called the solar system.
- The planets, the Sun, the moon and the stars together make up our universe.
- There are eight planets in our solar system. They are Mercury, Venus, Earth, Mars, Jupiter, Saturn, Uranus and Neptune.
- The moon moves around the Earth.
- Stars have their own light.

Exercises

A. Choose the correct answer to fill in the blanks.

1. .... is at the centre of the solar system.
   a. Mars   b. Sun   c. Earth
2. .... is the fifth planet from Earth.
   a. Mercury   b. Jupiter   c. Neptune
3. .... is the fourth planet from the Sun.
   a. Venus   b. Mars   c. Uranus
4. .... is the planet with life on it.
   a. Mars   b. Earth   c. Saturn

B. Write T for True and F for False.

1. The solar system has eight planets. ☐
2. Stars are smaller than Earth. ☐
3. The Sun does not move from its place. ☐
4. On a new moon night, a round circular moon is visible to us. ☐
5. The Sun is a star. ☐

C. Answer in one word.

1. Name the planet closest to the Sun. ....
2. Name the planet farthest from the Sun. ....
3. Name one planet that has rings around it. ....

Think Big

Art integration

Make your own rocket!

Material required: Toilet paper roll, craft paper, chart paper, glue, scissors and pencil

Method:

1. Take a craft paper and cover the toilet paper roll with it neatly.

2. Paste two round circles on the roll to make the body of the rocket.
3. Cut out a circle from the coloured chart paper and make a cone.
4. Cut out three stands, as seen in the picture, from the chart paper.
5. Make 3 slits in the bottom part of the toiled paper roll and fix the stands through the slits.
6. Glue the cone to the top of the roll to get the rocket shape.

Your rocket is ready to take off!

Learning Tools

Solve the word grid and find atleast 10 words on the solar system.

N	E	P	T	U	N	E	S	U	N
A	S	A	T	U	R	N	R	X	U
E	N	O	X	S	L	A	Q	F	R
S	R	J	S	T	V	U	W	Z	A
M	Z	U	Z	A	E	L	G	E	N
O	B	P	I	R	N	T	W	T	U
O	L	I	R	S	U	H	C	X	S
N	Q	T	B	N	S	M	A	R	S
S	M	E	R	C	U	R	Y	F	W
U	C	R	X	E	A	R	T	H	Q

Web links:

https://spaceplace.nasa.gov/
https://spaceplace.nasa.gov/menu/sun/

Last accessed on 30 August 2021

What is happiness?

Happiness is a combination of feeling good and satisfied with your day.

Let us do some fun activities.

A. Help Ria and Romi reach their homes from their school. Trace the path to their homes using two different colour pencils. Name one landmark near Ria's home and one near Romi's house.

B. Look at the picture clues and solve the crossword. Can you guess the special keyword?

C. Raj went to visit his grandparents who have a huge garden with a variety of fruit trees. Raj collected information on the fruit trees and then recorded it in the form of a pictograph as shown below:

Mango trees	
Orange trees	
Apple trees	
Cherry trees	
Plum trees	

Refer to the pictograph and answer the following:

1. Name the tree which is greatest in number in the garden.
2. Which tree is least in number in the garden?
3. Which two trees are of the same number in the garden?
4. How many fruit trees are there in the garden?

D. Solve the given code to get the names of the insects.

2 20 19 19 5 17 6 12 24

18 14 1 9 12

18 15 9 4 5 17

2 5 5

A = 1	F = 6	Q = 16	Y = 21
B = 2	G = 7	R = 17	W = 22
C = 3	H = 8	S = 18	X = 23
D = 4	I = 9	T = 19	Y = 24
E = 5	J = 10	U = 20	Z = 25

WORKSHEET

Worksheet (Chapters 13-16)

A. Answer in one word.

1. The weather, when there is a lot of wind ....
2. Festival celebrated in Kerala with boat races and rangolis ....
3. An area of lowland lying between two hills ....
4. A group of stars which forms a pattern ....

B. Write T for True and F for False.

1. Plains are areas of land surrounded by water on all sides. ☐
2. Trees shed their leaves in the autumn season. ☐
3. The Sun is one big ball of fire. ☐
4. Harvest festivals are celebrated to mark somebody's birthday. ☐

C. Fill in the blanks.

1. In places where it rains a lot, areas get .... with water.
2. .... festival celebrates the birthday of Lord Krishna.
3. Three-fourth of the Earth's surface is covered by ....
4. .... is the planet which is farthest from the Sun.

D. Solve the equations and colour the rangoli pattern.

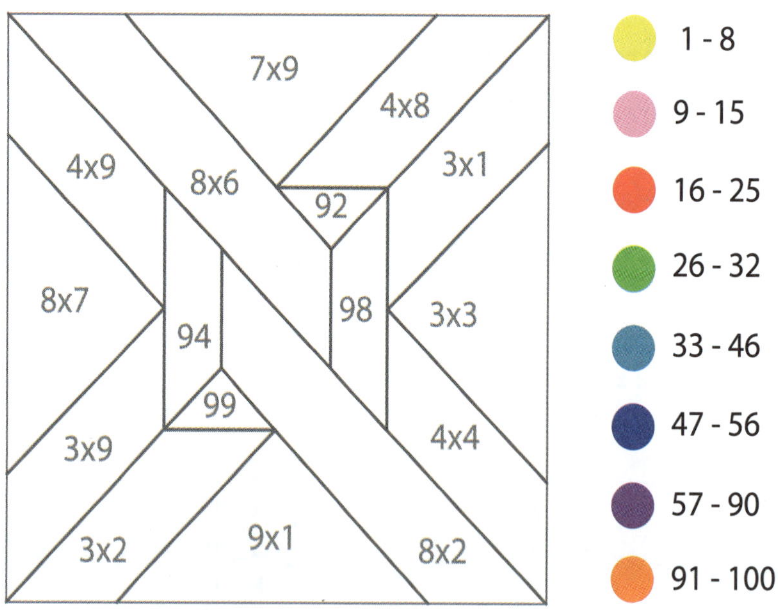

ASSESSMENT 1

A. Choose the correct option to fill in the blanks.

1. A healthy house must have ....
   a. fresh air b. pet animal c. table and chair
2. Pharmacy is a place where they sell ....
   a. fruits b. medicines c. books
3. An astronaut wears a ....
   a. raincoat b. space suit c. sports wear
4. .... is the main source of water.
   a. Pond b. Rain c. Tap
5. The parts of the body that are outside and can be seen are called .... organs.
   a. external b. internal c. sense

B. Solve the riddles.

1. This is something you can find
   In a lake and in a stream
   When frozen it turns to ice
   When boiled it turns to steam.

2. I am a body part
   But I am not a knee
   I am found on your face
   I am what you use to see.

3. If you're sailing on a pirate ship
   To find your way you'll need at least
   This item that will help guide the way
   By pointing north, south, west and
   east

4. Although these might get wet
   they are not things that will float
   they protect from the rain, heat and cold
   Made from different materials, they are
   ....

C. Match the following.

Column A	Column B
1. Police station	a. a place that covers and gives protection
2. Compass	b. an occurrence of a disease that affects many people over a very wide area
3. Pandemic	c. used for sharing direction
4. Occasion	d. place to contact when theft occurs
5. Shelter	e. an event or celebration

D. Write T for true and F for false.

1. Family members support each other during sickness. ☐
2. Pucca houses are temporary houses. ☐
3. People go to a shopping mall to fill fuel in the car. ☐
4. A clock is a device that gives us the exact time of the day. ☐
5. We need water to put out a fire. ☐

ASSESSMENT 2

A. Write T for true and F for false.

1. Air has speed
2. Fruits have seeds in them
3. Aquatic animals live in land
4. We must always wear a seat belt
5. Weather changes every day

B. Choose the correct option to fill in the blanks.

1. Animals living on trees are known as .... animals.
   a. domestic b. arboreal c. aquatic
2. An ambulance, a police car and a fire engine are all known as .... vehicles.
   a. small b. personal c. special
3. A flat land like a table top is called a ....
   a. plain b. plateau c. mountain
4. A cook wears a ....
   a. apron and a cap b. shirt and trouser c. coat and suit
5. We get cotton from ....
   a. animals b. grass c. plant

C. Circle the odd one out.

1. Rivers	Lake	Pond	Dam
2. Water	Roots	Leaves	Stem
3. Temple	Gurdwara	Church	Park
4. Tiger	Elephant	Parrot	Lion
5. Road	Rail	Water	Cave

D. Pick the right word to complete the paragraph.

planet need dirty clean liveable home

Earth gives us everything that we .... It gives us water, air, food, sunlight and many other things. We should take care of the .... and not .... it. If Earth becomes too dirty, it will not be .... Since this is our ...., we should keep it ....